IMMEDIACY AND ITS LIMITS

IMMEDIACY AND ITS LIMITS
A Study in Martin Buber's Thought

Nathan Rotenstreich
*Israel Academy of Sciences and Humanities
Jerusalem*

harwood academic publishers
chur • reading • paris • philadelphia • tokyo • melbourne

Copyright © 1991 by Harwood Academic Publishers GmbH, Poststrasse 22, 7000 Chur, Switzerland. All rights reserved.

Harwood Academic Publishers

Post Office Box 90
Reading, Berkshire RG1 8JL
United Kingdon

58, rue Lhomond
75005 Paris
France

5301 Tacony Street, Drawer 330
Philadelphia, Pennsylvania 19137
United States of America

3-14-9, Okubo
Shinjuku-ku, Tokyo 169
Japan

Private Bag 8
Camberwell, Victoria 3124
Australia

Library of Congress Cataloging-in-Publication Data

Rotenstreich, Nathan, 1914-
  Immediacy and its limits : a study in Martin Buber's thought / Nathan Rotenstreich.
      p.   cm.
  Includes bibliographical references and index.
  ISBN 3-7186-5108-4
  1. Buber, Martin, 1878-1965.   I. Title.
  B3213.B84R68   1991
  181'.06--dc20   91-31244
                                                                                    CIP

No part of this book may be reproduced or utilized in any form or by any means, electronic or mechanical, including photocopying and recording, or by any information storage or retrieval system, without permission in writing from the publisher. Printed in Singapore.

Contents

1	Introduction : Humaneness as Fulfilment	1
2	Background	5
3	Existence and its Basis	9
4	Trends and Topics	17
5	The Fellow and the Other	29
6	Horizon and its Hold	35
7	Ontology	39
8	The Encounter	49
9	Immediacy of Mediation	61
10	Faith and Reciprocity	75
11	Religion versus Philosophy	85
12	Reconsideration	99
Index		113

Author's Note

My point of departure for the present book is the prevalence of a basic theme and approach in Buber's thought—the immediacy of the interhuman encounter. I have tried to analyze that approach and its background both historically and conceptually.

One might argue that an attempt to deal analytically with that approach is essentially an expression of a critical attitude toward a phenomenon pointed to and described as given and present. The book tries to understand Buber's thought but does so critically. Because of the emphasis on the conceptual infrastructure, various expressions of Buber's thought, including social ideology, do not play a central role. The basic issues of his interpretation of religion, however, are dealt with.

Mr Arnold Schwartz took upon himself the editorial task. Unfortunately he passed away shortly after completing this work in the prime of his life. Blessed be his memory. The Lakritz Foundation of the Hebrew University, whose aim is to promote studies in Buber's thought, extended its assistance. My friends Professor R. J. Zvi Werblowski and Professor Paul Mendes Flor sponsored the decision taken by the Foundation.

I appreciate very much the openness of Harwood Academic Publishers and the help of Dr Gillian Rose who was kind enough to make comments on the manuscript. These have been included in the text.

Bibliographical Note

The texts referred to in this work are quoted from the following editions. The first reference is to the German original in the Lambert Schneider edition, Heidelberg 1984. After the title of the particular work the number of the volume is mentioned. The page number after the semicolon refers to the English translation.

The Question to the Single One
Education
What is Man?

are quoted from:

Between Man and Man, transl. by Ronald Gregor Smith (London: Routledge & Kegan Paul, 1949).

I and Thou, is quoted from the translation by Ronald Gregor Smith (New York: Charles Scribner's Sons, 1958).

Distance and Relation

Elements of the Interhumans are quoted from the *Knowledge of Man*; Selected Essays Edited with an Introduction by Maurice Friedman (Harper and Row Publishers, New York 1965).

Chapter One

Introduction: Humaneness as Fulfilment

[1]

Martin Buber was an explorer of human nature. At the core of his thought, even when he dealt with problems of religion and the concept of God, his concern was the human essence and man's position in the world. This is so even in his earliest writings before what is considered the turn in the development of his thought, such as his book *Daniel*, published in 1913. Although the theme of that book is the mystical experience, the union of man and God, Buber is also interested in what the mystical experience can reveal about human activity and nature.

Buber's anthropological explorations lead him to a view of what constitutes the fulfilment stage of human nature. Put simply this can be understood as the reciprocal relationship between man in the actual situation, and the moral ideal, subsumed under the term "I-Thou". The present work is intended as a critical analysis of Buber's view of the I-Thou relation considered to be the highest stage and fulfilment of human nature.

[2]

In *Daniel*, Buber elaborates the duality in Man's basic approach, or attitude, to the world. He speaks of "orientation" on the one hand,

and "realization" or "materialization" on the other. Kant describes the anthropological aspect of the philosophical concern as relating to what he called the "common experience". Indeed both attitudes described by Buber, orientation and realization, refer to what human beings encounter or experience in their everyday existence.

In the attitude of orientation, Man faces the world as given, or as a sum total of objects. Objects call for cognition which, at least ultimately, enables the person to find his way among the objects cognized. The encounter between the human person and the world in this attitude is inherently one of knowledge, including, and perhaps fundamentally, instrumental knowledge. Orientation is a functional and practical approach to the world, not simply for the sake of cosmological discernment *per se* but for the sake of day-to-day existence. It is not acknowledgement of the world as such; it is not based upon nor does it realize a symmetry between the human being and the world, for within it only the world as a sum total of objects is recognized; the person in his or her human context is not. In this sense, the attitude of orientation is a forerunner of the I-It relationship, in which the object is opposite but not in interrelation with the person.

In contrast, the attitude of realization is not primarily the cognitive attitude of an observer, but an involvement of the acting person in his surroundings with the purpose of bringing about change. It thus has more of an active component than orientation. Nonetheless, the cognitive component, though more prominent in orientation, is also present here; In neither attitude however, is there cognition for its own sake. This non-theoretical, or even anti-contemplative, ingredient was retained by Buber in the distinction he expounded later between the I-It and the I-Thou attitudes.*

Within the context of this distinction, cognition is more a feature of the I-It than of the I-Thou attitude. The cognitive approach to the world is less symmetrical than the broad involvement of the I in encountering the Thou, which is accompanied by the Thou encountering the I. Therefore, the cognitive relation, or in the terms of the previous stage of Buber's thought, the attitude of orientation, is

---

* In this exposition I have followed the chapter on Buber in the book by S. H. Bergman, *Dialogical Philosophy from Kierkegaard to Buber* (Jerusalem: Bialik Institute, 1974), an English version of which will soon be published. I have relied on that presentation not only because Bergman was my teacher but also because he was both a disciple and companion of Buber. His succinct presentation is both illuminating and authentic and thus serves as well as a point of departure, particularly as what follows in the present book is of a critical character.

less harmonious than the I-Thou relation. By the same token, the I-It relation is less of a fulfilment of human nature than the I-Thou relation.

We can take what have traditionally been called virtues, i.e. fidelity, friendship, or compassion, as the paradigms of the I-Thou relation. Buber placed these virtues within the context of his broader anthropological concern and regarded them as manifestations of humaneness. Humaneness manifested as friendship or compassion and characterized by the symmetry of the I-Thou relation is, in this view, the highest stage of human nature and thus its fulfilment. Empathy is regarded not as a sporadic attitude of human beings but is universalized as the fulfilment of their essence. Concurrently, it is presented as a norm for human beings. This is more than the intentionality that becomes manifest in the relation to objects, because intentionality, being a feature of consciousness, precludes the symmetry between the person and what is outside the person as an object. Intentionality refers to an object, and thus is one-sided from the point of view of Man. Buber observes that the physician is a physician only when he feels himself to be the patient whom he is attempting to heal. The attitude that may exist in encounters between the doctor and his patient when the Thou ceases to be just a case is taken by Buber to be both the fulfilment of human potentiality and the guiding principle of human existence and conduct.

[3]

Human potentiality figures as a theme in various anthropological approaches to human existence. In many of these approaches history is viewed as essential for deciphering human existence. History as a process in time is by definition a scene of potentiality. Since man transforms himself throughout history, the process exhibits his hidden potentiality. Buber, however, tries to place anthropological reflections within the dialogical, not the diachronic, context. For him the historical process is not essential to the identification of human existence, and cannot be seen as the scene of realization of the human essence or of the particular coexisting encounter between human beings inherent in the I-Thou relation. One of the reasons for this is that the historical process is, in a sense, anonymous. It may bring about the perspective of openness, but openness towards an undetermined future not the openness between two human beings.

Buber took the dialogical relationship further, transposing it from the human, or interhuman, context to the relation between man and God. He maintained that even the religious attitude expressed in the relation to God is dialogical. That is to say, God and man meet on equal terms or in stronger terms, God needs man as much as man needs God.

This brief statement of the fundamental theme present in Buber's thought is by means of introduction to the analytic interpretations and investigations taken up in this book. Some of the critical aspects have already been hinted at, for example the relation between analytic and normative components. But the basic theme throughout the following exposition is whether the I-Thou relation refers to immediate contact between human beings, as Buber saw it, or whether that relation is something established or aspired to. We will also consider the impact of the I-Thou relation on various aspects of human existence, such as language and the religious attitude.

Anthropology has been conceived as the doctrine of human nature. Kant thought that anthropology has to be based on the common human experience and not, for instance, on the findings of science. Looking from this description and anticipating Buber's conception of anthropology focusing on the interhuman relation we may say that the view as presented in Daniel contains seeds of Buber's anthropology. To be sure, the main issue of this book is not human interrelations but the two approaches to the world-orientation and realization. Looking at this distinction or duality from the later conception of the I and Thou, and I and Id, the difference of approach is indicative of the difference of the position of man within the human context. We notice also that in this book Buber tends to emphasize attitudes in a dualistic way giving preference to one of the ways as the fulfilment of human essence. The duality is described as such but the preference is granted to one of the directions contained in it. Hence, in spite of the duality the attitude preferred is both an expression of human essence as well as the norm of human existence and conduct. The harmony of that which is given and that which is called to be the principle of preference of human essence is present already in Daniel and becomes the focus of the later development of Buber's thought. This will be our concern in the following exposition. The given components of the human essence are not only the anchor or the norm but are essentially identical with it. This major topic will be further analyzed in the following discussion.

Chapter Two

Background

[1]

Looming in the background of Buber's thought are some philosophical problems related to knowledge and to the phenomenon of language. Though they do not feature directly in Buber's exposition of his thought, their illumination is a useful first step with which to begin our undertaking.

The first issue that ought to be examined is the anti-Cartesian direction that has developed in modern thought. Cartesian thought accorded priority to cognition or thinking. "Cogito" is a primary act. It enables the syllogistic conclusion affirming the existence of the thinking subject, and radiates its primacy on the establishment of existence or reality, at least in terms of the subject concerned. The anti-Cartesian trend that developed mainly in the eighteenth and nineteenth centuries sought to reject the primacy of cognition as an activity establishing reality.

Friedrich Heinrich Jacobi (1743–1810) was one of the first links in the chain of philosophers directed against the Cartesian attitude. In his view, both the external world and the I are given to us in an immediate manner requiring neither reflection, representation nor a discursive drawing of consequences. In this view, thinking is not the source of the substance; on the contrary, something which is not thinking is bound to precede thinking, and can be assumed as to be the first step.

Since cognition is inherently related to the I, the hard core of the anti-Cartesian argumentation is the attempt to negate not only the primacy of cognition but also the primacy of the I. Jacobi takes that step. He says "...without the Thou the I is impossible."* The priority attributed to the Thou over the I is, it seems, inherent in the priority of the immediate encounter over cognition and its alleged syllogistic consequence. Jacobi's assumption seems to be that the Thou has priority over the I within the immediate encounter, since the Thou is part of the surrounding world which is encountered directly or experienced immediately.

Buber follows Jacobi's anti-Cartesian line in taking immediacy as the essence of the relation to reality and human existence. Yet he does not posit the Thou as prior to the I. He attempts to present the Thou and I as encompassed together in the sphere of the "in-between". The I and Thou enter into a symmetrical relation in which the identification of the I is related to the identification of the Thou, and vice versa. To be sure, we can ask about the step taken from the "in-between" to the respective status of the two partners — the I and the Thou. While both of them are involved in the "in-between" sphere, each of them has an independent or semi-independent status.

Jacobi's emphasis on the priority of the encounter with reality over isolation is related to his general position on the attitude towards what goes by the name of the external world, the world beyond the I. Jacobi does not assume that the existence of objects outside the self, which are considered to affect our awareness, could be proven — the line implied by Kant. The objects of our awareness, Jacobi holds, are not merely phenomena. They are real objects and to break free from the assumed confinement of cognition to representations (*Vorstellungen*) or phenomena, a non-analytical approach must be taken. This approach is described by Jacobi as belief. We may assume that Jacobi took the presentation of belief as related to practical philosophy from Kant and transplanted it to the realm of knowledge interpreting knowledge not as a construction but as immediate awareness of that which is present. This enabled him to overcome the confinement of cognition or knowledge to the phenomenal world, and by the same token to posit an immediate relationship between awareness and the reality of the outside world. A thread of continuity can be discerned in Jacobi's own writings from a relation to belief as a manner of conception as formulated by Hume to his more extreme view in which belief results in the certainty of reality.†

---

* *David Hume über den Glauben, oder Idealismus und Realismus*, 1786, pp. 87, 199.
† This direction was characterized in the polemical presentations of

Buber accepted the trend that explicitly or implicitly denied the possibility of cognitive proof of reality. He also affirmed the immediate awareness of reality, though he confined these aspects to the relation between the I and the Thou, including the Thou of God. The immediacy of Jacobi's belief becomes in Buber the immediacy of the interpersonal contact. This leads to another direction implicit in Buber's thought related to language.

[2]

Broadly speaking, even as a mode of individual expression, language is an interpersonal resource or, as we say, a medium. The term "medium" immediately suggests communication, and communication entails an interhuman or interpersonal direction. We remain within the realm of communication even when we refer to language in terms of its descriptive function, for our descriptions are presented either to ourselves or to our fellow men.

A mode of linguistic expression relevant to our discussion, the dualis, was analyzed by Wilhelm von Humboldt. The dualis is a mode in which the speaker and person spoken to (*angeredet*) are always posited together as a unity. Humboldt traces it in many languages and finds it to be a variant of plurality that involves two persons, I and Thou (he uses those terms). The dualis refers also to pairs of natural objects like eyes and ears, but also stars.

Every act of speech, says Humboldt, is based on mutual speech in which speaker and addressee are posited as a unity. Such a dualism belongs to the original and immutable essence of language; the very possibility of speaking is conditioned by address and response. Only through the mediation of language can the connection between the other and the I emerge. Indeed, all the more profound and subtle feelings, the feelings that become prominent in friendship, love, and

---

nineteenth-century philosophy as a philosophy of not-knowing or as philosophy of feeling, and was developed by Dilthey in his essay on the external world. See: W. Dilthey, "Beiträge zur Lösung der Frage vom Ursprung unseres Glaubens an die Realität der Aussenwelt und seinem Recht" (1890), in: *Gesammelte Schriften*, Band 5 (Stuttgart-Gottingen: Teubner, 1974), pp. 90ff. Although Dilthey takes exception to Jacobi's view, the immediate approach to reality is also the prevailing attitude in his explanation.

all spiritual community between two persons, are conditoned by language.*

Applying the distinction common in present-day linguistics or philosophy of language between langue and parlance, we can say that parlance as an activity is the original link or contact between human beings. In this sense, it is a precondition for the various modes of attachment and contact between them. The linguistic affinity between human beings serves Buber as a kind of a paradigm for assessing the various contacts between the I and the Thou. It cannot be said that these contacts emulate language, but language is present both explicitly and in the various modes of correlations between human beings, which in turn are similar to the linguistic contact exhibited in parlance.

Even though language is originally a formulated expression, a primary immediacy is presumed to be inherent in linguistic contact. That is to say, the immediacy of the contact does not annul the formulation as the explicit medium of contact. Transposing this description to the I and Thou in the general sense, we can say that neither the I nor the Thou as persons disappear in the contact between them, or, to put it differently, they are not brought into a sort of mystical union. They exist in correlation and their primary correlation is made explicit by the immediate contact which links them together. In our explorations of the various topics of Buber's thought we shall see that the aspect of immediacy is central to his various presentations and analyses. At the same time, this aspect leads us to some critical observations.

---

* Über den Dualis, in: Wilhelm von Humboldt, Werke, herausg. von Albert Leitzman, vol. VI, Erste Halfte, (Berlin: B. Behr's Verlag, 1907), pp. 17, 25, 26, 27. Buber mentions Humboldt's treatise in his Zwiesprache (p. 169), and refers to it as significant.

Chapter Three

Existence and Its Basis

[1]

The phenomenon of "dialogical life" is the constant theme of Buber's thought. It is also his main contribution to what might be called an ontology of human life. In the course of his development Buber introduced several terms for describing this phenomenon, such as dialogue, essential relation, the "between". Though there is a slight shift in emphasis in the various terms, the essential idea is retained: the primacy of interrelation within the human scope.

Following Buber's own description, we may say that the sphere of the interhuman is that of persons vis-a-vis one another; the explication of this sphere is called the dialogical form (*'das Dialogische'*).* To be in the vis-a-vis situation is to be embedded in, or to have entered into, mutuality.† The partners in a situation of mutuality, those usually termed as "I" and "Thou", are established through the relation of mutuality: "I become through my relations with the *Thou*; as I become I, I say *Thou*."‡ A possible interpretation of this statement might be that the whole comprising the interrelated human beings is more than the sum of its components. However Buber actually wants to place the emphasis not so much on the independence of the whole as on the independence of the relation between the components rather than that between each of the individual components. "Each, considered

---

* *Elemente des Zwischenmenschlichen*, vol. 1, p. 272; p. 74.
† *Über das Erzieherische*, vol. 1 p. 791; p. 81.
‡ *Ich und Du*, vol. 1 p. 85; p. 11.

by itself, is a mighty abstraction. The individual is a fact of existence insofar as he steps into a living relation with other individuals... the fundamental fact of human existence is man with man."*

This sphere of "between" is not simply given and established once and forever. It is created time and again in the course of human life, but even so it is more than just a product of those creating it. The very creation of mutual contact between human beings is said to presuppose a kind of instinct toward this creation inherent in human beings.

> "Between" is not an auxiliary construction, but the real place and bearer of what happens between men; it has received no specific attention because, in distinction from the individual soul and its context, it does not exhibit a smooth continuity, but is ever and again re-constituted in accordance with men's meetings with one another.†

The most characteristic feature of the "between" is just this, that it is both concrete and "airy". Because of the combination of these two aspects, it is difficult to articulate the interhuman scope conceptually. Furthermore, the bias of the prevailing systematic forms of philosophical thought, in our age at least, is towards analysis of wholes and relationships, an analysis which amounts to reduction and hampers the assessment of the independence of the sphere of the "between".‡ Buber himself uses the expression "mysterium" in this context, and thereby heightens the difficulty of a morphological, let alone conceptual, establishment of the sphere of the "between".

According to Buber, the essential relationship between two human beings is the new phenomenon introduced into the cosmos by the appearance of man. The fact that there are human beings gives rise to a primordial chance of being, and it is of this which Buber speaks.§ It might be added that Buber does not always confine his description and analysis to the human sphere proper, as for instance when he says, describing the emergence of answer or response: "A dog has looked at you, you answer for its glance."¶ Nonetheless, his main concern is with the nature of relationship within the human sphere, and the allusions to what is beyond this sphere are simply an expansion of his major findings about the character of the human sphere.

---

*   *Das Problem des Menschen*, vol. 1 pp. 405–406; p. 203.
†   Ibid.
‡   *Elemente des Zwischenmenschlichen*, vol. 1 p. 279; p. 81.
§   *Nachwort*, vol. 1 p. 191.
¶   *Zwiesprache*, vol. 1 p. 191; p. 35.

[2]

One major concrete expression of the existence of the sphere of the "between" is the phenomenon of answer: "...a word demanding an answer has happened to me."* The fact that "answer" points to a dialogical situation may be why Buber uses the term "dialogue", though, as we shall see, Buber himself goes beyond the sphere of linguistic expressions. Still, it might be said that the experience of being addressed and answering, "a word and response",† is the focus of the sphere of the "between" or, to put it differently, it is the appearance in life of the essence of the mutual "between".

The living contact established in the situation of address and response leads Buber to a further step: that of stressing the phenomenon of responsibility in its two senses — responding to an actual call of one person and response as a normative requirement. The second sense approaches responsibility as it has been discussed in the philosophic and juristic literature, that is to say, responsibility *qua* accountability. Yet because responsibility even in this latter sense is presented by Buber not as being required to account for one's deeds, omissions and so on, but as being required to live up to the real and essential level of human life — that of responding to a fellow man — responsibility ceases to have a narrow meaning or, for that matter, a moralistic one. Buber suggests that such responsibility is rooted — and manifested — in the fundamental features of human life. To put it differently, responsibility has a broad meaning because it is not placed in the impersonal domain of action nor is it seen as serving a standard idea of the actions one is supposed to perform; for example, having to be honest according to an idea of honesty. Responsibility is placed in the realm of responding to an independent human being or, in Buber's own words: "Responsibility presupposes one who addresses me primarily, that is, from a realm independent of myself, and to whom I am answerable."‡ The fact that Buber uses the expression "answerable" points to the second sense of responsibility: being required to act in a way that accords with the essence of human life, which is mutuality; in this case mutuality amounts to responsibility. We might say that in order to stress that a human being can be bid to behave in a certain way, Buber has to use a "dispositional" expression

---

*   Ibid., p. 183; p. 29.
†   *Die Frage an den Einzelnen*, vol. 1 p. 222; p. 66.
‡   Ibid.

namely that human beings are potentially responsive and resposible. Yet he formulates the dispositional aspect through his main idea, that it is to say the essence of human beings is to respond, because responsibility is ultimately rooted in the nature of the human sphere.

It has been said that dialogue is the focus of the sphere of the "between". We may now add that responsibility is the focus of dialogue. As responsibility is rooted in dialogue, dialogue is rooted in the very essence of human life. These aspects are conjoined possibly because Buber strives for an ontological or anthropological warrant for the ethical aspect of responsibility. As he himself says: "The idea of responsibility is to be brought back from the province of specialized ethics, of an 'ought' that swings free in the air, into that of lived life. Genuine responsibility exists only where there is real responding."*

This attempt to provide an ontological warrant for ethics is actually an attempt to "ethicize" the human sphere in its essence. The scholastic idea of *ens et bonum convertuntur* ("being and good are interchangeable") is realized, at least primarily, within the human sphere. Human beings embedded in the relationship of mutuality are "persons" in the terminological sense of the word because of this intrinsic ethical aspect of the sphere of the "between".

Scheler observes that human beings are unities of their experiences and not merely thinking entities behind and beyond what they actually experience. Buber implies much the same when he says: "The I of the primary word *I-Thou* makes its appearance as person and becomes conscious of itself as subject."† This would seem to mean that the unity of experience is established only in the actual meeting with a fellow human being; that is so because the unity of experience is established in experience itself, and this in turn is living actuality only in the sphere of the "between". Hence the status and character even of personality is established in the sphere of human mutuality.

[3]

Buber himself does not employ the terminology of the ontological warrant for the ethics of mutuality. Yet the idea is implicit in various expressions he uses to establish the primacy of mutuality. For in-

---

*   *Zwiesprache,* vol. 1 p. 189; p. 33–34.
†   *Ich und Du,* vol. 1 p. 120; p. 62.

stance: "In the beginning is relation — as category of being, readiness, grasping form, mould for the soul, it is the *a priori* of relation, the *inborn* Thou."* The synonymous use of "inborn" and "a priori" in this quotation reflects a combination of Kantian and pre-Kantian philosophical traditions. That in itself is not as important as the fact that in his search for a way to establish mutuality as the essence of human existence, Buber adopts epistemological terms like "a priori" or "inborn". What he actually wants to emphasize is the idea that mutual relations between human beings are an irreducible fact, or a sphere *sui generis*. He expresses this by saying that "The inborn *Thou* is realised in the lived relations with that which meets it. The fact that this Thou can be known as what is over against the child... is based on the a priori of relation."†

This statement seems to imply a duality within Buber's morphology of human existence: there is the "inborn Thou" and the Thou as realized. Buber probably assumed that he eliminated the impasse of that duality because the mutuality intrinsic to the human sphere is incapable of being analyzed to its components. Mutuality is irreducible. Yet if it is said that the Thou is inborn, it follows that the mutuality can be dismembered, that is to say, there is an I with an inborn Thou and there is an actual or empirical Thou, and there is the realization of that relation within the actual sphere of human existence. The persistence of this duality is an outcome of Buber's attempt to base mutuality on a fundamental datum: sometimes he assumes that mutuality itself is a fundamental datum and sometimes he roots it in the inborn capacities of the individual human being. Nonetheless, it might be said that the main idea is that in the beginning there is relation and that relation cannot be explained even by an a priori or inborn Thou.

In a later stage of his thought, Buber speaks of the "*innate* capacity in man to confirm his fellow man" [emphasis added].‡ His oscillation between the primacy of relation and the innateness of the approach to the fellow man has some bearing on philosophical problems implied in Buber's thought. These will be dealt with presently.

---

*   Ibid., p. 96; p. 27.
†   Ibid.
‡   *Urdistanz und Beziehung*, vol. 1 p. 420; p. 28.

[4]

A slightly different way of stressing the primacy of the relationship with one's fellow man is the employment of the term "instinct", as in the following: "What teaches us the saying of *Thou* is not the originative instinct but the instinct for communion."[*] Here again Buber appears to introduce a term in order to establish the reality of the mutual relationship between human beings as an ultimate fact. The status of ultimate fact is expressed by the term "instinct". Still one may doubt whether the "instinct for communion" introduced here is an adequate description of what Buber is trying to convey. By rooting the factual and overt reality of human life in an instinctive urge of human beings, an explanation of communication, or of being in communion, as an inherited instinct of human nature is a subjectivist approach. If relation is the primary sphere, the individual human being is created in and through relation, and the instinct for communion cannot be independent of actual communion as a primary fact.

If Buber's use of the terms "a priori" and "inborn" reflects the influence on him of epistemological strains of thought, his employment of the term "instinct" may be seen as his obeisance to the psychological vogue. This is seen in the following statement:

> This instinct is something greater than the believers in the 'libido' realize: it is a longing for the world to become present to us as a person, which goes out to us as we to it, which chooses and recognizes us as we do it, which is confirmed in us as we in it.[†]

The idea of "longing" also conveys a subjective urge and might be a trace of a kind of romanticism. Again, it is doubtful that it adequately represents Buber's own phenomenology of human existence. Buber wants to show that the sphere of "between" overcomes subjectivism, or as he himself puts it: "A transfusion has taken place after which a mere elaboration of subjectivity is never again possible or tolerable to him."[‡] But terms like "longing" retain connotations of subjectivity.

Surveying the advantages of the primacy of mutuality, according to Buber, one may say that in the first place the dichotomy of collectivism and individualism is thereby overcome, as, in a parallel manner, subjectivism is supposedly overcome:

---

[*] *Über das Erzieherische*, vol. 1 p. 789; p. 114. The German term is Urheber*trieb*.
[†] Ibid.
[‡] Ibid.

> I am speaking of living actions, but it is vital knowledge alone which incites them. Its first step must be to smash the false alternative with which the thought of our epoch is shot through — that of "individualism or collectivism." Its first question must be about a genuine third alternative.*

And further:

> Individualism sees man only in relation to himself, but collectivism does not see man at all, it sees only "society." With the former man's face is distorted, with the latter it is masked.†

The third alternative Buber has in mind is obviously that of the "between", where man is not related only to himself nor is he submerged in an anonymous society. Further still: "... as there is a *Thou* so there is a *We*."‡ "Only men who are capable of truly saying *Thou* to one another can truly say We with one another."§ "Marx did not take up into his concept of society the real relation between the really different I and *Thou*."¶ It is because of this distinction that in later presentations Buber is careful to distinguish between social life and the sphere of the "between", and assumes that he thereby transcends the traditional sociological distinction between society and community, *Gesellschaft* and *Gemeinschaft*. The real dichotomy is not between society and community but between society as an aggregation of particular and isolated human beings and the *We*, the plurality of human beings presented through the grammatical form of the first person plural. The *We* is not primarily given as are the I and the Thou in their mutual relation, but is an outcome of the factual relationship. Although what is traditionally called community might be considered a closer realization of the reality of *We* than society is, the two are not identical. *We* is ontologically closer to the proper realm of human existence, that of mutual relationship.

Another advantage of the primacy of dialogical mutuality might be its ethical aspect, which is related to the idea of responsibility dealt with earlier. "Trust, trust in the world, because this human being exists — that is the most inward achievement of the relation in education."**

---

* Ibid.
† Ibid., p. 450; p. 241; pp. 243–44.
‡ Ibid. p. 411; p. 213.
§ Ibid.
¶ Ibid., p. 365; p. 182.
** *Über das Erzieherische*, p. 281; p. 125.

Though the notion of trust is introduced here in the context of education, it seems proper to interpret it as the manifestation of mutuality in general. Buber's is the ethics of trust or confidence, and these attitudes in turn are manifestations of responsibility *qua* addressing and being addressed. This reflects an optimistic strain in Buber's thought, which has some bearing on the general tenor of his outlook. But in this context it will suffice to say that because mutuality is a primary feature of human existence, non-involvement in mutuality as an experience and reality can only be regarded as a deviation or displacement from fundamental facts. The ethical attitude of trust, by contrast, is an active manifestation of the factual basis and nature of human life.

Ultimately, there is a congruence between the phenomenological, ethical and religious view as Buber sees it. Criticizing ethics as isolated from the morphology of human existence, he says:

> Religion certainly, has this advantage over morality, that it is a phenomenon and not a postulate, and further, that it is able to include composure as well as determination. The reality of morality, the demand of the demander, has a place in religion, but the reality of religion, the unconditioned being of the demander, has no place in morality.*

The anti-Kantian innuendo that can be heard here is central in Buber's position because he relates responsibility to somebody calling for response.

The ethic of responsibility is amplified by the notion or, in Buber's own view, the reality of an ultimate demander. That is to say, he points to the idea of mutuality not only within the confines of the human realm but also, and perhaps most significantly in the first place, within the scope of the relationship between man and God. The argument seems to be this: since mutuality is actualized in responsibility, and responsibility presupposes two partners in dialogue, there is a demand to transcend the human sphere in the confined sense of the term and reach a super-human personality as the dialogical partner, as the demander and super-human Thou. We shall return to this in our analysis of faith.

---

* *Zwiesprache,* pp. 155–56; p. 36.

Chapter Four

Trends and Topics

[1]

Buber usually omits historical references and is little concerned about his thought's location within an historical-philosophical context. If we are to understand the trend of his thinking, however, we must attempt to situate it in its proper context beginning by considering some individual philosophers.

The philosopher perhaps most quoted and referred to in Buber's writings is Feuerbach. Buber criticizes Feuerbach for removing God and in His place, apotheosizing the human relation between an I and a Thou, and for, what he calls, the postulative trend in his thinking. Feuerbach formulates the demand for the radical renunciation of the concept of God, substituting an anthroplogical concept for it. Buber describes Feuerbach's view as a "pseudo-mystic construction."* Nonetheless, he is aware of the relationship in which he stands to Feuerbach — particularly the latter's emphasis on man in his relation with his fellow man, and perhaps also with regard to a further point not stressed by Buber, namely, that even in one's thinking, that is to say in one's position as a philosopher, one remains a concrete human being, a man among men.† But even though Buber feels indebted to Feuerbach, the differences between them are major — not because of the postulative character of Feuerbach's thinking (does Buber's think-

---

*   *Nachwort*, vol. 1, pp. 288, 289, 309.
†   L. Feuerbach, "Grundsätze der Philosophie der Zukunft", in: *Säm. Werke*, Vol. 15, ed. by W. Bolin and Fr. Jodl (Stuttgart: Fromman, 1904), p. 318.

ing lack postulates?), nor even because of the anti-theological character of Feuerbach's thought, but because of differences in their respective fundemental metaphysical position.

The difference between Buber and Feuerbach can perhaps best be expressed in this way: Feuerbach emphasizes the relation between the I and Thou because he objects to idealism, while Buber focuses on this relation because his first and greatest interest is the scope of human reciprocity. The main point in Feuerbach's philosophy seems to be the shift from philosophical distinctions, including that of subject and object, to what he considers to be sensual — and therefore immediate — distinction. The most prominent of the latter is that which exists between the I and the Thou. As Feuerbach himself puts it, the secret of immediate knowledge is sensuality.* We might say, then, that while Buber attempts to be *concrete*, Feuerbach identifies concreteness with *sensuality*. The target of Feuerbach's attack is the philosophy of identity, which, in his view, nullifies the immediate distinctions. This is not unlike Buber's attack against doctrines and philosophies that do not place the relation between concrete human beings at the center of their systems. Feuerbach's, however, is a comprehensive system of thought, whereas Buber presents variations on one theme — I and Thou — and has no intention of creating a system.

Buber observes that in spite of the difference between his own thought and Kant's philosophy there is an affinity between them.† He sees the difference in the fact that Kant confines his conception of the human being to the ethical realm: the human being is an end in itself. We have seen before that though Buber's own view is certainly to a very large extent colored by ethical considerations, he is critical of any abstract ethical position. Yet he seems to think that he provides a foundation for the ethical view. According to Kant, the position of man as an end is grounded in the very relationship between the human being and the ethical sphere, that is to say in the very fact that the human being is rational and hence responds to the ethical imperative. Buber presents the position of man as an end through its realization within the human scope, that is to say, within the texture of the relation between the I and Thou and not against the background of reason: since the human being is in the first place embedded in a dialogical situation he is bound to be considered as the end and not the means. It is questionable whether the philosophical foundation

---

*   Ibid., p. 301.
†   *Elemente des Zwischenmenschlichen*, vol. 1 p. 276; p. 84.

suggested by Buber for the status of an end is sufficient, as he is inclined to think.* Reason is capable of establishing the position of man as human being precisely because it is not confined to the dialogical situation between two human beings. By way of contrast, the dialogical situation, limited as it is to two persons and not to man as human being, would seem not to have that capability.

In his later writings, Buber stresses the affinity between his analysis and that presented by Hermann Cohen, who in his later period said that only the discovery of the Thou leads one to consciousness of one's own self.† Yet one may question whether such an affinity really exists, because Cohen does not maintain that the *meaning* of the relationship between the I and Thou is primary, immediate and given. On the contrary, even in his later period Cohen retains what can be called the objective trend, stressing that though the I and Thou are given in experience and from this point of view are natural data, their religious value depends upon their being elevated to their status only in the moral sphere. Actually, even in Cohen's later writings the moral and religious position of the Thou, though not its givenness itself, is deduced from reason. This can be seen in his emphasis on the importance of pain and poverty for the position of the Thou. Pain is the bridge between the I and Thou and the concrete manifestation of pain is poverty; or as Cohen has it, poverty is the optical means for putting the human being into relief as a Thou and thus as a natural object of man's love.‡ Buber, by contrast, does not stress any specific embodiment of the encounter between two human beings in order to perform, as it were, a philosophical deduction of the position of the Thou. Buber is certainly more immediate, more experiental and more intuitive than Cohen was even in his later writings. Here too Buber's ways of reasoning differ from those of the philosophers he mentions as kindred thinkers.

---

*   His affinity to some trends in Fichte's doctrine has been pointed out in H. Bergman, "Begriff und Wirklichkeit, Ein Beitrag zur Philosophie, Martin Buber and J.G. Fichte," *Der Jude* (Berlin, 1928). Buber himself does not extensively discuss Fichte's systems.

†   *Nachwort*, p. 290.

‡   See: Hermann Cohen, *Der Begriff der Religion im System der Philosophie* (Giessen, 1915), p. 79; see also the present author's: *Jewish Philosophy in Modern Times: From Mendelssohn to Rosenzweig* (New York: Holt, Reinhart and Winston, 1968), pp. 52 ff. deals with the issue.

[2]

If we wish to identify the philosophical tradition in which Buber's thinking is rooted, we must refer to some kind of *Lebensphilosophie* — though not in the technical sense of the term — and to some kind of intuitionism, again not in the technical sense.

A quotation from one of Buber's major works may suffice to indicate his kinship with the general atmosphere of *Lebensphilosophie*: "Lived life is tested and fulfilled in the stream alone."* This statement would seem to indicate Buber's intention to remain, as it were, in the stream of life and to give a philosophical account of the experiences of human life from within, that is to say, from the position of life itself. This being his intention, it is not surprising to find a kind of scepticism in his writings not only toward philosophical systems, but toward the philosophical attitude in general. As he says: "I did not rest on the broad upland of a system that includes a series of sure statements about the absolute, but on a narrow rocky ridge between the gulfs where there is no sureness of expressible knowledge but the certainty of meeting what remains undisclosed."† Statements of this sort, expressing scepticism or reservation with regard to philosophical systems, were common in the philosophical tradition of *Lebensphilosophie*. More important, however, is that in speaking about philosophizing and philosophy, Buber stresses that these are primarily acts of abstraction.‡ This is not merely a description but a criticism of an abstract attitude, which removes us from "the stream of life". Criticizing the attitude of abstraction, Buber says: "Here you do not attain to knowledge by remaining on the shore and watching the foaming waves, you must make the venture and cast yourself in ... in this way, and in no other, do you reach anthropological insight."§ What here is called "anthropological insight", and is set in opposition to abstraction, is grasping the stream of life from within. It might be mentioned here that philosophy of intuition uses the very same argument against remaining on the shores in the stance of a spectator. It presents intuition as participation in the stream of life, and views conceptual knowledge as an expression of an outsider position removed from

---

*   *Zwiesprache*, p. 148; p. 30.
†   *Das Problem des Menschen*, p. 424; p. 223.
‡   Religion and Philosophy, in: *Eclipse of God* (New York: Harper and Row, 1952), p. 38.
§   *Das Problem des Menschen*, vol. 1 p. 329; p.155.

that stream. Buber is strongly connected with that trend, possibly to an even greater extent than he himself is aware.

[3]

Buber does deal explicitly with Bergson's interpretation of intuition. He is critical of Bergson for not stressing the special position of the Thou, rather than the universe at large, as a primary reality, and says that without acknowledgement of the primary reality of the Thou, intuition is merely a patchwork of diverse components. Buber is aware of the weakness of intuitionism, namely that in an act of intuition one may become submerged in the moment without reaching the true reality of the intuited object, which lies beyond the present moment in which the intuition is performed.* Nonetheless, he seems to share the intuitionist view of the non-cognitive, or rather non-conceptual, attitude that exists between two human beings and establishes their relationship. But he criticizes intuitionism because of the "cognitive atomism" that threatens it, the possibility that every act of intuition might be unrelated to the former or subsequent act. He also criticizes it because of the lack of clear realism in, at least, some intuitionist views: Buber is strongly interested in stressing the independent, i.e., realistic, position of both partners in the dialogical situation, and the contact established in and through intuition may lead to the blurring of the independence of both the I and the Thou.

In spite of this difference between Buber's view and the mainstream of intuitionist philosophy, a number of expressions found in his writings reveal the intuitionist character of his thinking. There are some terminological inconsistencies, mainly in the use of the word "experience". In one context, for instance, experience is placed within the I-It as opposed to the I-Thou relation, thus stressing the difference between experience and mutuality,[†] while in a different context, to stress the immediate contact, Buber speaks of one person "experiencing" another.[‡] But this is a minor terminological quibble. There are, however, usages whose intuitionist connotations are unquestionable.

---

* See on this his Hebrew article "Bergson and Intuition," introducing a selection of Bergson's writings, *Spiritual Energy* (Tel Aviv, 1944); partially translated as "On Bergson's Concept of Intuition," in: *Pointing the Way*, pp. 81–86.
† *Ich und Du*, p. 18; p. 6.
‡ *Zwiesprache*, p. 134; p. 19.

One example is the use of the term *"personale Vergegenwärtigung"*.[*] This kind of "personal making present" is a summing-up of various recurring descriptions in Buber's writings of immediate knowledge of the Thou. "The world of *Thou* is not set in the context of either of these [i.e., space and time];"[†] — and even stronger: "What does he now 'know' of the other? No more knowing is needed. For where unreserve has ruled, even wordlessly, between men, the word of dialogue has happened sacramentally."[‡] Because the immediacy of the approach to the fellow man is stressed, Buber says: "Only when every means has collapsed does the meeting come about."[§] This direct relation to the Thou is called essential relation. It is described: "The two participate in one another's lives in very fact, not psychically but ontically."[¶] Buber himself avoids the term "intuition" but he employs terms remininiscent of intuitionist descriptions; for instance, *participation* ("participation in the existence of living beings,")[**] or *inclusion* ("through inclusion of one another by human souls.")[***] He even draws a distinction between empathy and inclusion:

> Empathy means, if anything, to glide with one's own feeling into the dynamic structure of an object... as it were, to trace it from within... it means to 'transpose' oneself over there and in there.Thus it means the exclusion of one's own concreteness, the extinguishing of the actual situation of life, the absorption in pure aestheticism of the reality in which one participates. Inclusion is the opposite of this. It is the extension of one's own concreteness, the fulfilment of the actual situation of life, the complete presence of the reality in which one participates. Its elements are, first, a relation, of no matter what kind, between two persons, second, an event experienced by them in common, in which at least one of them actively participates, and third, the fact that this one person, without forfeiting anything of the felt reality of his activity, at the same time lives through the common event from the standpoint of the other.[****]

Empathy for Buber is not realistic enough because it tends to blur the independent position of the two human beings meeting each other in a dialogical situation. The emphasis is on the meeting that takes

---

[*]   *Elemente des Zwischenmenschlichen*, p. 270; p. 78.
[†]   *Ich und Du*, p. 44; p. 33.
[‡]   *Zwiesprache*, p. 135; p. 20.
[§]   *Ich und Du*, p. 12;
[¶]   *Das Problem des Menschen*, p. 403, p. 207.
[**]   Ibid., p. 495, p. 238.
[***]   *Über das Erzieherische*, p. 280; p. 124.
[****]   Ibid. pp. 280–281; p. 124.

place between two distinct human beings. Stressing the danger inherent in empathy as an exclusion of one person for the sake of his or her partner, Buber introduces his own term: inclusion. Close to "intuition", the term "inclusion", like similar terms introduced by Buber, is meant to stress the immediate relation between the two human beings: "Opinions were gone, in a bodily way the factual took place."* Because of the emphasis on the immediacy of the awareness, Buber, like the intuitionists, speaks of knowing with one's whole being: "The primary word *I-Thou* can only be spoken with the whole being. The primary word *I-It* can never be spoken with the whole being."† In a different context, where Buber seeks to describe the forces underlying the immediate encounter, he introduces the term "real imagining" (*Realphantasie*),‡ which again calls for emphasis on the first part of the term, "real", but goes beyond knowledge in the discursive sense.

[4]

In this intuitionist tenor of his thinking, Buber is close to his teacher, Dilthey. In a later writing, when Buber speaks of perceiving the wholeness of another human being, he talks of perceiving that person's dynamic center and being aware of all the manifestations of that human being in attitude and deed.§ This penetration to the center of the human being is similar to what Dilthey called awareness of the structural context of the soul or of the living context of action. Such awareness requires a specific cognitive medium, namely insight or what Dilthey called *Verstehen*.¶ Buber, one may say, refers to the real situation which calls for *Verstehen*. But the relation of mutuality between human beings is not only a cognitive situation — cognitive though supra-conceptual. It is first of all a living situation, in which the cognitive approach, be it participation, inclusion, etc., is embedded. Historically speaking, it may be said that Buber intended to provide an ontology of human relations in which *Verstehen* is not only legitimate but also a necessary and exclusively adequate cognitive mode. The causal or descriptive attitude toward psychic life, which

---

*   *Zwiesprache*, p. 138; p. 22.
†   *Ich und Du*, p. 15; p. 3.
‡   *Elemente des Zwischenmenschlichen*, p. 212; p. 78.
§   Ibid., p. 270.
¶   See: Wilhelm Dilthey, Ideen über eine beschreibende und zergliedernde Psychologie (1894), *Werke*, 5 (Stuttgart: Teubner, 1924), p. 206.

had been the focus of Dilthey's critique, reappears in Buber's thought in his discussion of the "primary word *I-It*," which calls for a different cognitive attitude from that of the "primary word *I-Thou.*"

A realistic approach is tied up with the intuitionist strain in Buber's thinking. He expresses his realism in two ways: in the ordinary sense while speaking about communication among human beings as they really are.* In this sense he is anxious to state that the immediate approach between human beings includes their mutual awareness free of the epistemological distinctions between appearance and reality. The immediate approach thus breaches, as it were, the walls of mediation and discursive thinking. From this point of view it can be said that Buber tries to overcome the solipsistic predicament through the device of the philosophy of the dialogical situation. He presents the idea that the human being is primarily interwoven in the situation of meeting his fellow man. This meeting is not given lacking awareness; it is not opaque; it is understood *qua Verstehen*. Thus the ontological situation of the dialogue is *ipso facto* an epistemological situation of mutual and adequate knowledge.

In another sense his realism has the meaning of everyday life and everyday knowledge. "I possess nothing but the everyday out of which I am never taken."[†] Criticizing modern trends in philosophy, Buber says that "the man of modern philosophy who pretends to think in reality and not in ideation — does he think in reality?"[‡] The fact that Buber appeals to everyday life as an authority for knowledge and as a field which has to be accounted for in a philosophical analysis is, of course, not unrelated to the intuitionist tendency of his thought, which this fact merely stresses from a different angle. To put it differently, Buber, like Franz Rosenzweig, appeals to everyday knowledge as opposed to ideation, though unlike Franz Rosenzweig he does not appeal to common sense but to what he calls "everyday". This, however, might be only an insignificant terminological difference. Like Franz Rosenzweig, he seems to think that what is "everyday", or common sense for that matter, has unambiguous meaning and has only to be stated. As such, it does not call for, and even precludes, a philosophical interpretation.

---

* "...mitteilen als das was sie sind." *Elemente des Zwischenmenschlichen*, p. 200; p. 75.
† *Zwiesprache*, p. 150; p. 32.
‡ Ibid., p. 170.

[5]

Proceeding in our analysis of the motives of Buber's thinking, we should consider what might be regarded as an optimistic strain in his thought. We refer to Buber's philosophical conviction that in the final analysis man is not a lonely being in the universe. Hence his view can be described not only as dialogical but also as dialogical cosmism. Let us examine this strain in his thought in some detail.

Firstly, this is one of the main points in Buber's polemic against Kierkegaard:

> A God in whom only the parallel lines of single approaches intersect is more akin to that "God of philosophers" than to the "God of Abraham and Isaac and Jacob." God wants us to come to Him by means of the Reginas he has created and not by renunciation of them.[*]

The meeting between God and man, it can be said as a positive conclusion from this polemical observation, occurs in the coming together of human beings and not in their lonely or solitary position. God wants us to affirm, not renounce, the living creatures with whom our lives are interwoven.[†] The immediate meeting of a single human being with God would amount to acosmism, that is to say to annihilation of the creation as it has been granted by God.

The affirmation of God seems to lead to the conclusion that we are called to affirm the human beings with whom we live, and this affirmation is decisively, even primarily, expressed in the dialogical situation.[‡]

> "An education based only on the training of the instinct of origination would prepare a new human solitariness which would be the most painful of all."[§]

Buber's objection is to leaving the human being in his solitary state, which is akin to Pascal's fear of infinite space. In his anthropological writings Buber considers that anthropological awareness is the ontological-philosophical expression of the existential situation of solitary state. He, however, wants to combine anthropological awareness with what he calls a "new house in the universe."[1] He seems to think

---

[*] *Die Frage an den Einzelnen*, . p. 207; p. 52.
[†] *Nachwort*, p. 289.
[‡] Here we find the explanation of Buber's rejection of mysticism, because in his view mysticism amounts to acosmism.
[§] *Das Problem des Menschen*, p. 347.

that the philosophy of the dialogical situation is an adequate assessment of the specific human situation and allows it to be rooted in the universe. The dialogical situation is, as it were, a microcosm of habitation within the cosmos. It mediates between individual human life and the cosmos at large, or put differently, it overcomes from the beginning the loneliness of the human being.

Buber is, of course, aware of the alternative view represented by Spinoza's or Hegel's philosophy: that the link between the human being and the universe is mediated by thinking. Against Hegel's view he says: "The Hegelian house of the universe is admired, explained and imitated; but it proves uninhabitable. Thought confirms it and the word glorifies it; but the real man does not set foot in it."*

This criticism of Hegel is close to that expressed by Franz Rosenzweig. Buber seems to think that to be related to the universe in a positive and affirmative sense is to live in it in the simple sense of the word, and to live is to live with other human beings. Thus, a cosmic attachment is provided in and through the medium of the situation of the I and the Thou and not through speculative thinking as held, for example, by Spinoza and Hegel.

Buber, in other words, sees the inner connection between what he calls cosmic and social homelessness.† He seems to think that overcoming social homelessness — the homelessness nearest to the concrete human being — through dialogue leads *ipso facto* to an overcoming of cosmic homelessness. In the same way overcoming cosmic homelessness in the dialogical situation between the human being and God leads to the overcoming of social homelessness in the dialogical situation between one person and another. This is the optimism inherent in Buber's thought, the belief that the same device can overcome both social and cosmic homelessness. This optimism is rooted in his idea that the primary human situation is also the normative principle and guide for what human life ought to be. The problematic situation of modern man, or the "sickness of time," as he puts it, is an indication of our alienation from the basic and normative human situation, a deviation from the primary situation which has been forgotten, or abandoned, and must be restored.

---

* *Über das Erzieherische*, p. 266; pp. 87, 114.
* Ibid., p. 352–353, p. 173.
† Ibid., p. 450; p. 241.

[6]

One of the roots of Buber's thinking is to be found in his criticism of the contemporary situation, of our "times of sickness."* He himself tells us that in the period of the First World War or, as he calls it, the time of the Vesuvian hour (*vesuwishe Stunde*), a general trend arose which he characterizes as a strange longing to do justice to existence by thinking.† Thus, for instance, he regards the separation between spirit and instincts, which he finds both in Freud's psychology and Scheler's anthropology, as an indication of the more fundamental separation between man and man, man and God, or man and the cosmos.‡ To take another instance, he considers Heidegger's philosophy to be based on the isolation of one realm of man, that of the isolated individual human being, from the wholeness of life.§ In short, the contemporary spiritual situation seems to be one of disregard for the dialogical forms in the narrow human and broad religious sense. The analysis of the contemporary situation is performed by means of dialogical philosophy, and at the same time that analysis is one of the driving forces in the formulation of that dialogical philosophy.

Having explained some affinities and differences between Buber's thought and trends in philosophical thinking, we turn now to an examination of specific issues.

---

* *Ich und Du*, p. 65; p. 53.
† *Nachwort*, 1954, p. 290.
‡ *Das Problem des Menschen*, p. 198; 447–448; p. 239.
§ Ibid., p. 400; p. 205.

Chapter Five

The Fellow and the Other

[1]

Buber wishes to establish a two-way relationship between the human being and God: the human being is not totally submerged in God but stands vis-a-vis Him as an independent or semi-independent partner; furthermore, God too is independent and not just an element of subjective experience. The awareness by human beings of this relationship between man and God, based on the independence of the two partners, may be Buber's underlying "philosophical intuition" as well as the driving motive for his general view of mutuality.

This view, which enlarges the scope of mutuality to include the encounter between the human being and God, is not without its ambiguities. Within the confines of the human sphere mutuality, as we have seen, is fundamental and must be regarded as the ontological basis of human life. But when Buber asserts mutuality also in the encounter with God, we cannot but wonder as to the relationship between these two mutualities. Is it Buber's claim that besides mutuality in the human sphere there is a mutuality between man and God independent of the former, or does he wish to establish the idea of mutuality in general, asserting that it is realized both within the confined human sphere and in the meeting between the human being and God? It seems that Buber himself offered no definitive word on this issue, which can be regarded as the systematic issue par excellence of his thought.

In one version of his view he says: "The extended lines of relations meet in the eternal *Thou*."* This might suggest the idea of projection from the human sphere toward the meeting with God. According to this suggestion the primary fact is the meeting between the two partners within the human scope. This meeting is extended beyond the human scope through the approach to God in His position as the eternal Thou.* Yet Buber also says that "in each *Thou* we address the eternal *Thou*." This statement implies that the eternal Thou is present, inherent or hidden, within the human scope. The extension of the lines is in the nature of an explication of what is inherent or implicit rather than an extension in the sense of leaving a confined sphere. But he also says, "The relation with man is the real simile of the relation with God."†

This seems to suggest that the relation with God is the primary fact while the relation with man is but an expression or human manifestation of the primary relation with God. In yet another rendering of this idea it is said that the Thou encountered in the relation between man and man is the same as that which comes down to us from God and ascends from us to God.‡ According to this version, the idea of the Thou is the primary idea, and it has a twofold realization - within the human sphere and in experience of God. The variety of renderings might be understood, and to some extent rightly so, as reflecting Buber's own struggle for the most adequate expression of his major intuition.

[2]

Yet within this variety of renderings lurks a real philosophical problem: because Buber does not want to establish the Thou as merely an abstract notion, a kind of Platonic Thou, as it were, appearing in various experiential phenomena, he has to demonstrate the unity of the essence and reality of the Thou as a fundamental and irreducible fact of human experience. This is the difficulty inherent in his attempt to unify what he calls theological anthropology and philosophical anthropology. On the one hand he is eager to maintain the metaphysical presupposition of the concrete man's bond with the absolute,§ as

---

*   *Ich und Du*, p. 83; p. 75. The book *I and Thou* is central in Buber's thought and development. See: Robert E. Wool, *Martin Buber's Ontology, An Analysis of I and Thou* (Evanston, Ill.: Northwestern University Press, 1969).
*   Ibid., p. 18; p. 75; p. 6.
†   Ibid., p. 111; p. 103.
‡   *Nachwort*, p. 299.

he himself puts it, while on the other hand he still wants to deal with human existence as it is experientially realized in the mutuality of "between". The trend toward unification of the two possible experiences leads him to systematic oscillation between asserting the semi-independence of the human sphere and man's experience vis-a-vis God, and establishing a synthesis of the two experiences. The former view, if maintained, might lead ultimately to an affirmation of the two distinct avenues of experience, which amounts to a hesitation as to whether mutuality within the human sphere is actually a primary ontological fact, as might be programatically asserted. Maintaining the latter view might bring Buber to the problem of whether the relationship to God is an extension of the human sphere or, conversely, the human sphere is a confinement or limited realization of the primary relationship with God.

Buber does not deal with the ontological problem confronting his view on this point to a sufficient extent for us to reach a conclusion as to his position. It seems that here too the shift toward experience enables him to avoid raising the ontological problem and to remain within the experiential encounter itself.

> All the enthusiasm of the philosophers for monologue, from Plato to Nietzsche, does not touch the simple experience of faith, that speaking with God is something *toto genere* different from 'speaking with oneself'; whereas, remarkably, it is not something *toto genere* different from speaking with another human being.*

The ontological problem as to which is primary, the meeting between human beings or that between the man and God, is put, as were, to one side, while the similarity of the experiences in both spheres is stressed. But even if, for the sake of discussion, we grant that the experiental aspect can be dealt with apart from the ontological problem, it remains questionable whether this similarity can be maintained. Within the human sphere the problem can arise of out of the interpretation, i.e. the problem of whether or not we actually encounter a Thou, as in the various discussions on the epistemological question of the identification of the other not just as a mute datum but as a human being. Now, if the problem of interpretation arises within the human sphere, it arises even more so in the sphere of the experience of God as the absoluteness of the Other, to use Buber's own

---

§ *Das Problem des Menschen*, p. 391; p. 199.
* *Die Frage an den Einzelnen*, p. 204; p. 71.

words.* "Human life," says Buber, "touches on absoluteness in virtue of its dialogical character."† This appears to be less a feature of human experience or intuition than an interpretation of human experience, and perhaps one that aspires towards its total systematization as present in philosophical systems. If God is the absoluteness of the Other, then the idea of otherness is introduced into the system depending on what is taken as primary, either as an amplification of the other encountered within the human sphere, or as an absolute warrant for the independent position of the other. It might be noted that absolute otherness as a warrant for the independence of the other being occupies a position parallel to that of "thing in itself" in Kant's view, at least one of the functions of which is to safeguard the reality of appearances, or to ascertain their givenness vis-a-vis reason or intellect.

In the idea of God as understood by Buber we again find a combination of the two characteristics of otherness in the human sphere, independence and relation: God is a reality independent of man and exists in a relation with man. But even assuming a parallel structure of independence and relation in both the human sphere and in the sphere of the experience of God, the problem of which structure is primary has to be raised, precisely in view of what Buber says about mutuality as a fundamental feature of human life.

[3]

The parallelism between the human sphere in the narrow sense of the word and the sphere between the human being and God appears to break down at one point. Within the human sphere the relationship between I and Thou can deteriorate to that between I and It. The deterioration is understandable, even if not ontologically or ethically justified. But within the sphere between the human being and God the introduction of the category, or primary word as Buber puts it, of *I-It* is not at all justifiable. God cannot be reduced ontologically to the level of an It because God is otherness in its absoluteness. "If God is addressed as He or It, it is always allegorically. But if we say *Thou* to Him, then mortal sense has set the unbroken truth of the world into

---

* Religion and Modern Thinking, in: *Eclipse of God*, p. 67.
† *Das Problem des Menschen*, p. 399; p. 204.

a word."* Could we assume that within the confined human sphere the status of He or It is but an allegory?

We may now suggest the following interpretation. The position of God as the absolute other is not only a warrant for the position of the fellow man as an independent and related other. It is also the ideal of otherness in the personalistic and ethical sense of the word. Buber may have been reluctant to accept this interpretation because it sounds like an idealistic interpretation of the otherness of God, being both an idea and an ideal. Yet, paradoxically, Buber's view of God comes close to an idealistic position. Here one comes upon a gap between his "philosophical intuition" and its exposition. To conclude we may say that the objective of Buber's thought was to establish the unity of religious experience and anthropological philosophy. As we have seen, it is by no means certain that this objective was attained.

---

* *Ich und Du*, p. 107; p. 99.

Chapter Six

Horizon and its Hold

[1]

The later stage of Buber's thought, expressed in his idea of distance and relation, leaves us with some doubt whether relationship within the human sphere is as primary as it was described in his earlier and more well-known work. To be sure, Buber uses expressions which reminding us of the context of his basic views such as, the expression "becoming a self for me" (*Selbst-werdung-für-mich*).[*] Yet in the later stage there is a kind of "second thought" as to the primacy of relationship as an independent, self-contained form of human existence. One of the indications of this revision of his position is that he begins to talk about a "primal setting at a distance" being "the presupposition of the other (entering into relation)." He continues:

> That the first movement is the presupposition of the other is plain from the fact that one can enter into relation only with being which has been set at a distance, more precisely, has become an independent opposite. And it is only for man that an independent opposite exists.[†]

These expressions point to a reflective attitude because to be removed from needs and wants is to maintain a kind of an overview of the basic situation. This overview in turn can be maintained only through reflection. When Buber talks about setting at a distance he is not talking in spatial terms but in terms of release, the latter being a

---

*   *Urdistanz und Beziehung*, p. 36; p. 71.
†   Ibid., p. 11; p. 60.

kind of freedom inherent in the position of a spectator. A looker is at a distance and because of that he reflects on his position and its setting. The attitude of a person in the position of a spectator is again reflective. If this interpretation is correct, then in his later stage Buber became aware of the fact that the experimental view he maintained in his major works is not independent and self-contained but necessarily rooted in a reflective attitude. How that attitude gets realized in the encounter is a topic which Buber did not analyze, though he maintains the duality of distance and mutuality. Distance is a position acknowledged by the I — but it does not involve mutuality. The world is a horizon which I and Thou fill. But the world is not active in the mutuality of human beings. Buber is bound to distinguish in this context between awareness and that which is there in spite of the fact that the intentionality of the awareness does not refer to that what is surrounding, as it were, it. We face here one of the limitations of a conception based on the immediate encounter. As experience presupposes, without being able to state it within the boundaries of itself, something which is not encountered, so the mutuality of relation presupposes a broader scope of reality than that present in it as such.

The notion of an independent opposite is retained from Buber's previous writings about the fellow man; God too, is still viewed as an independent opposite. But what is new is that Buber now seems to think that the position of being an independent opposite is not given or encountered originally within the human context. Instead, it is established through a specific attitude, that of setting a distance. Formally one may still argue that "setting at a distance" is a sort of relation. But as it was interpreted by Buber, relation was fundamentally a mutual relationship and its expression has been viewed as the contact of responsibility. From this point of view, relationship had from the outset a humane and even ethical connotation. But the relation of distance, to keep to the formal aspect, has different features and that is because here Buber explicitly transcends, as it were, the human situation. The question he is now asking is: where is the human situation placed, or where does the mutual relationship comes into existence? He answers: "Distance provides the human situation, relation provides man's becoming in that situation."*

If we consider the difference between a picture frame and the picture within the frame, we could say that in his later stage Buber wondered about the frame in which the picture of human life was set.

---

*   Ibid., p. 20; p. 64.

The picture itself is still of mutuality but it is explained through its placement in the context of the universe, and for the sake of this placement Buber introduces the notion of setting at a distance. But if this is so, then mutuality within the human sphere has ontological primacy only *prima facie*, because ultimately the setting at a distance, or the presence of distance, is the ontological presupposition of the sphere of relationship, and thus of mutuality. The fact that Buber in a way enlarges the locus of the human situation is expressed as a corollary to the fact that now, following the biological distinction between the environing world (*Umwelt*) and the world at large (*Welt*), he speaks of a world that exists as an independent opposite through the setting of distance.* The mutuality of human relations is thus placed in the world. This being so, the world ceases to be a neutral, impersonal fact to be understood according to the category of It. If the world set at a distance is the presupposition of mutual relationship, we are actually going beyond the former rigid distinction between the primary words I-Thou and I-It. The world is not just an It and the relationship between I and Thou is not simply given. Being the presupposition of relations, the world now has a human meaning.

[2]

While introducing the idea of setting at a distance, Buber actually presupposes the fundamental position of reflection. To set at a distance is to maintain a reflective attitude. As Buber himself says, "It is only the realm which is removed, lifted out from sheer presence, withdrawn from the operation of needs and wants, set at a distance ..."† These expressions point to a reflective attitude because to be removed from needs and wants is to maintain a kind of sovereignty toward the basic situation. This sovereignty in turn can be maintained only through reflection. When Buber talks about setting at a distance he is not talking in spatial terms but in terms of release, the latter being a kind of freedom inherent in the position of a spectator. But the attitude of a person in the position of a spectator is again reflective. If this interpretation is correct, then in his later stage Buber became aware of the fact that the experiential view he maintained in his major

---

* Ibid., p. 23; p. 63f.
† Ibid., p. 149; p. 61.

works is not independent and self-contained but necessarily rooted in a reflective attitude.

Buber's experiential attitude breaks down, in a way, in the religious trend of his thought. There the direction is toward a combination of an idea and an ideal, as we have pointed out. Here the experiential trend of his thought is broken by the anthropological trend, that is to say, because he questions his own ideas on the presupposition for mutuality. In so doing, he questions the primacy of mutuality if not from the point of view of the genesis of our experience, then from the point of view of its ontological and logical foundations. The reflective attitude impinges and Buber, intuitively perhaps, thus touches upon the question of the transition from the reflective attitude to the mutuality of relationship. Here we come upon one of the most important critical points in Buber's thought, to which we will return later in the analysis.

Chapter Seven

Ontology

[1]

Our concern in this critical examination of some of Buber's ideas, is not the factual importance of the relation between one human being and another. We are interested, rather, in elucidating the basic ontological position of this fact in terms set by Buber himself, who claims to be inquiring into the basic stratum and texture of human existence. Regardless of the importance of human mutuality on the factual level, it is doubtful whether the factual level is metaphysically independent, whether it reveals the most fundamental level of human existence. In other words, the identity between factual importance and ontological relevance should not be taken for granted.

From the outset Buber identifies and deals with reality either as manifested in the relation between the I and Thou or as manifested in the relationship between the I and It. As he himself puts it: "*Real* existence, that is real man in his relation to his being, is comprehensible only in connection with the nature of the being with which he stands in relation."[*] Yet, as a matter of principle, a distinction has to be maintained between the concept of reality and reality as it is materialized in this or that field. We have to retain this duality and not assume, as Buber tacitly does, that the concept of reality divorced from its realization in a material field is merely an abstraction. To be sure, Buber shares the realistic and even existentialist bias of some modern trends of philosophy; he wishes to give an account from

---

[*] *Dialogisches Leben*, p. 393; p. 200.

within life and assumes there is neither way nor justification for dealing with reality other than by pointing to a specific field understood as reality. He says this, for example, in his discussions on the reality of the external world. But to identify any field of material data as reality, be it the external world or the mutuality between the I and Thou, one has to apply the concept of reality; the concept as such is not given with or in the field of the material data. Hence, the concept of reality is broader than that of a material realization of it. In other words, to know about the reality of the I and Thou we have to know about more than this particular reality.

Mutatis mutandis, the same can be applied to the concept of relationship. In order to identify this or that as a field of relationship, we have to presuppose the general concept of relationship and read it into a field of a concrete realization of relationship. Only then can we consider whether relationship is primarily realized in the sphere of I-Thou or in the sphere of I-It, granting the existence of these spheres.

This might sound like a scholastic or epistemological consideration with a Kantian ring, but that is not the purpose of this observation. The purpose is to show Buber's own ambivalence with regard to the reflective attitude. He himself is not clear as to whether reflection is an extraction from the primacy of mutuality or whether mutuality presupposes reflection. Earlier we showed that in one of his later works Buber decides on a reflective attitude as a presupposition for relationship. Some kernels of this later development, though not a clear conclusion on this point, can even be found in his earlier writings, for example in the book *I and Thou*

[2]

On one fundamental issue Buber holds a twofold view. He assumes that "through the *Thou* a man becomes *I*,"[*] or as he also says: "the *I* emerges as a single element out of the primal experiences, out of the vital primal words *I-affecting-Thou* and *Thou-affecting-I*, only after they have been split ..."[†] According to this view, there is a primary wholeness of the I in its relationship to the Thou, but at the same time the particular I is but a result of an isolation from the comprising wholeness. Thus we may ask what kind of isolation is performed here

---

[*]   *Ich und Du*, p. 40; p. 28.
[†]   Ibid., p. 33; pp. 21–22.

and by what means? Is it like the falling away of a piece of stone from a conglomerate of sand, that is to say, an isolation in space? Or is it self-realization of the I through its awareness that it differs from the Thou, from the whole of the relationship, that is to say, self-realization through reflection? Does the I emerge as a self because the center of its existence is rooted in reflection? While he recognizes the primacy of relationship over the independence of the I, Buber does not seem to share the notion of the importance of the reflective attitude as a basic condition for the self-awareness of the I as an independent entity:

> ... man's essential life is not to be grasped from what unrolls in the individual's inner life, nor from the consciousness of one's own self, which Scheler takes to be the decisive difference between man and beast, but from the distinctiveness of his relations to things and to living beings.*

At this point it has to be asked whether the specific features of the spheres of relations can be assumed without presupposing the status to the consciousness of one's self. There is a decisive reason for this: if we do not grant the consciousness of one's own self the status of being imbued with characteristics of its own, we face the riddle of how a human being could realize that it is he or she as a human being who maintains relations to things and to fellow beings. The human being is not just submerged in the wholeness of relation; rather, his or her position amounts to a twofold attitude of detachment and attachment, both aspects simultaneously present. But it is not possible to be both detached and attached without the consciousness of one's self as a constitutive feature or factor in the total situation, as Buber himself later recognized in his idea of setting at a distance as an outcome of a reflective attitude.

Buber applies a metaphor to express his point, but what he says metaphorically hardly contributes to a conceptual elucidation of his objective: "Life is not lived by my playing the enigmatic game on a board by myself, but by my being placed in the presence of a being with whom I have agreed on no rules for the game and with whom no rules can be agreed on."† But is this the real dichotomy — being placed on the board by oneself or being placed in the presence of another? The position of being placed in the presence of another being

---

*   *Das Problem des Menschen*, p. 448; p. 240.
†   Ibid., p. 396; p. 202.

does not abolish the position of the self. It is myself, as a self, that is placed in a certain position, and ultimately consciousness is the basic foundation for my self-awareness as "myself". Furthermore, there is no real dichotomy between being placed in the presence of another human being and playing according to rules. It matters little whether or not rules are of prime importance in the relation. Even if we grant that rules are secondary because they are limited, or because they do not exhaust the total field of relationships, there is still a fundamental difference of roles between the I and Thou. This division is not the result of game rules; it is a manifestation of the self-consciousness of each of the two human beings in the relation.

Hence one may doubt whether Buber does justice to Heidegger's view of the essence of man, even if one takes a critical stance toward Heidegger's philosophy. Buber says on Heidegger:

> ... the anthropological question, which the man who has become solitary discovers ever afresh, the question about the essence of man and about his relation to the being that is, has been replaced by another question, the one which Heidegger calls the fundamental-ontological question, about human existence in its relation to its *own* being.[*]

Again the critical question has to be posed whether this — the relation to one's own being and the relation to the fellow man — is a real dichotomy. The two relations can be considered as being on two different levels. Heidegger's ontological question refers to the position of self-consciousness; hence he talks about the ontological sphere as different from the ontic sphere. Buber, however, identifies human existence in relation to one's own being with solitariness, as if the two were identical. But the basic stratum of self-consciousness does not make human beings solitary; it merely points to the center and focus of all man's relations, including those with fellow men or with the world in general. Without the presupposition of self-consciousness, all relations would split up or dissolve into atomic moments without the continuity of human relations. To be sure, Buber is aware that, as he describes them, human relations are difficult to grasp because they might exhaust themselves in a present of flowing and disappearing actions. Though this impressionistic drift is implicit in Buber's view, he tends to support a notion of continuous creation in the field of human relations. Yet there is no other condition for the existence of

---

[*] Ibid., p. 398; p. 204.

such ongoing creation save for the fact that at the center of human relations is the self-consciousness of the partners involved in them.

[3]

Our purpose until now has been to show that Buber assumes the primacy of relations over the independent status of the I. But, as the following quotations from his writings show, he also holds the contrary view: "Certainly in order to be able to go out to the other you must have the starting place, you must have been, you must be with yourself."*

Distinguishing between the psychological primacy of the relation with the Thou and the status of the I as an independent being, he declares: "It is true that the child says *Thou* before it learns to say *I*; but on the height of personal existence one must truly be able to say *I* in order to know the mystery of the *Thou* in its whole truth."† Though there is no explication of the mystery of the Thou in this context, one might guess that it is related to the existence of the Thou as an independent human being, which is to say one centred in its own consciousness. In opposing what he calls the "height of personal existence" to the psychological process of the development of consciousness, Buber in effect points to the distinction that has to be drawn between the psychological and factual level of human existence (the developmental process) and its ontological and logical roots and conditions. Buber's own oscillation between the two views, i.e., the primacy of the relationship and the primacy of the I, reflects his own hidden oscillation between a factual description of human life and his intended ontology of it.

One may wonder however, whether Buber's account of the emergence of the consciousness of the I within the setting of the relation with the Thou is even factually adequate. Here is the outcome of a psychological or psychopathological examination, which is not to be taken dogmatically but is an indication that should be taken into consideration:

> The need for nature was strongly anchored in her. After the walk (and the following imposed rest) she usually occupied herself more readily

---

*   *Zwiesprache*, p. 106; p. 39.
†   *Das Problem des Menschen*, p. 410; p. 212.

> and in a better way. It even made her more sociable, while curiously enough, forced contact with people caused her to withdraw within herself. Apparently the pleasure found in nature gave her narcissistic strength...[*]

It can be argued that the above quotation refers to a forced contact with people. But it seems that the main question is whether the forces for the emergence of a stable I are to be found within the scope of the mutuality between human beings or whether they have to be grounded — at least partially — in the relationship between the human being and nature or the human being and the universe, as some thinkers have assumed. To be sure, this is a factual psychological consideration, but since Buber draws on factual psychological insight, the factual question raised here might be considered not out of place in our discussion. One possible conclusion would be that the transition from factual findings to an ontological conclusion cannot be accepted without reservation.

We move to a further critical observation, not unrelated to the former one: the question must be asked as to whether the outcome of Buber's thinking is a philosophical description of the human situation or an establishment of normative postulates and imperatives of what human life ought to be. Buber cannot avoid the postulative bias, though as mentioned before, he criticizes Feuerbach for his postulative attitude. Buber says:

> We should live not towards another thinker of whom we wish to know nothing beyond his thinking but, even if the other is a thinker, towards his bodily life over and above his thinking — rather towards his person, to which, to be sure, the activity of thinking also belongs.[†]

Though this is certainly a postulate, even stylistically, a broader issue arises in this context. We may grant that the fulfillment of human existence is to be found in the mutuality of human relations, and suppose that the mutuality of human relations is a kind of *entelecheia* of the features of humankind. But it does not follow from this that the human being must be defined fundamentally as a creature of mutuality. There is no contradiction — as seems to be supposed by Buber — between one's relation to oneself in a reflective attitude and one's realization in the mutuality of human relations.

---

[*] Margaret A Sechenhaye, *Symbolic Realization* (New York: International Universities Press, 1951), p. 113.
[†] *Zwiesprache*, p. 170; p. 47.

[4]

It was said before that if human relations are not rooted in self-consciousness, they may become atomic, momentary, ephemeral. Only by grounding them in reflection, or self-consciousness, do we step beyond the factuality of the flow of changing relations. Buber, however, does not wish to ground relations in a realm such as self-consciousness or in a specific content that might overstep the relations themselves. Even the relationship with God does not overstep going beyond the confined scope of relationships proper, and for that reason does not establish something substantive that is not just the dynamics of relationship but also a content of relations. Though Buber talks about dialogue and dialogical situations, dialogue as a dynamic occurrence in the plane of linguistic expressions is actually just a metaphorical description for him: "Real faith ... begins when the dictionary is put down, when you are done with it."[*]

It is not by chance that Buber stresses the overcoming of linguistic expression, because in a linguistic expression there is something that refers to a reservoir of actually conveyed contents. But the doctrine of dialogical mutuality is not based on the notion of a substance or a content that is conveyed in the dialogical meeting. According to Buber, the very dialogical meeting is, as it were, its own content, or as he puts it: "Consider man with man, and you see human life, dynamic, twofold, the giver and the receiver, he who does and he who endures."[†] In this dialogical situation there is a giver and a receiver, but no realm of content is given or received, because the very situation is considered to be self-contained, or as Buber has it, "the Eros of dialogue has a simplicity of fullness."[‡]

It can be understood why Buber tries to avoid the world of substantive content. He seems to think that the assumption of a realm of content would amount to an introduction of a screen between the two human beings meeting each other, and thus would abolish the immediacy of their meeting and being together. Hence he says: "Spirit is not the *I*, but between *I* and *Thou*... Man lives in the spirit, if he is able to respond to his *Thou*."[§] Here again one may doubt whether this is a real dichotomy i.e., either spirit inherent in the I or spirit inherent in the relation between the I and Thou. The view that we are referring

---

[*] Ibid., p. 141; p. 29.
[†] *Das Problem des Menschen*, p. 458; p. 247.
[‡] *Zwiesprache*, p. 172; p. 49.
[§] *Ich und Du*, p. 49; p. 39.

to some principles, like that of the truth or of the good, leads us to a transcendence of both the I and the I-and-Thou. But Buber attempts to avoid transcendence of the scope of relations for a third realm of contents. "Man receives and he receives not a specific 'content' but a Presence, a Presence as power;"* or, in a different context, "divine Presence, for this Presence's becoming dialogically perceivable."† This statement is highly relevant to Buber's religious thinking: in his view revelation does not express itself in content but only in the givenness of the Presence or in the meeting with the Presence without the medium of a content and without crystallization in a content.

Leaving aside the religious aspect of his thinking, one may wonder whether any human situation, or any situation at all, is self-contained in the dynamics of active relations and as such is not included in a framework of content or is without a kernel of content as its constitutive factor, as Buber seems to think. This is so not only because ideas and interpretations cannot be avoided, but also because in a dialogical situation one acknowledges a human being in his position as a human being. This acknowledgement itself is not immediately given or evidently imposed upon us. Rather it presupposes the idea of human existence or the conception of the human being as human person, a notion which is only partially realized in the partners meeting each other. To put it differently: any meeting between human beings that carries with itself the acknowledgement of oneself and one's fellow as concrete human beings is bound to be accompanied by the notion of man as man. Analogous to what was said before, that the identification of a field of reality presupposes the idea of reality, it can now be said that the identification of a dialogical situation presupposes the idea of the human being — hence a content or a third realm beyond relations and the individuals involved in them.

[5]

In a way, Buber deals with this problem when he says: "Appeal to a 'world of ideas' as a third factor above this opposition will not do away with its essential twofold nature."‡ But the purpose of our

---

* Ibid., p. 118; p. 110.
† "God and the Spirit of Man," in *Eclipse of God*, p. 126.
‡ *Ich und Du*, p. 25; p. 13.

critical observations is not to do away with any justified twofold nature but only to point out that the scope of relations is not self-contained. It refers to factors that are not in themselves in the nature of relations, such as principles, ideas, etc. This conception is criticized by Buber when he speaks of:

> the fictitious responsibility in face of reason, of an idea, a nature, an institution, of all manner of illustrious ghosts, all that in its essence is not a person and hence cannot really, like father and mother, prince and master, husband and friend, like God, make you answerable.*

Paraphrasing Hegel, we could say that the realm of reason, ideas, etc. is considered to be fictitious not because of its intrinsic nature but because one considers it to be so. Only if we assume that human existence exhausts itself in personal relations are we led to the view that whatever transcends personal relations is actually fictitious. But here too the dichotomy — this time either personal relations or fictions — can be called into doubt. Although reason is a principle, or the level of awareness of principles, and thus is not a personal factor, there is reality in reason and we are answerable to it. We are answerable to the principle of truth, though the principle of truth is not like father and mother, nor even like God. We are answerable to reason, because reason is a precondition even for relations. We are also answerable to it because the dynamics of relations are not unguided, and are, or at least may be, restrained, shaped, channelled. The tension between dynamics and guidance expresses the relation between our spontaneous activities and the principles to which we are answerable.

The elimination of a third realm, be it of concepts like reality, spirit, and principles, leads Buber to what might be called metaphysical impressionism. This can be shown at least at one point: "The present arises only in virtue of the fact that the *Thou* becomes present."† Of the full span of time Buber is bound to acknowledge only the present, and temporal presence is but an expression of existential presence, be it of a human being or of God, devoid of substantive content. But while human existence flows through and actualizes itself in the present moment, it is not just a collection of these moments. Situated between reflection and principles, it also has continuity. Buber's obliviousness to these two realms, reflection and spirit in the substantive sense of the word, is an outcome of the postulative nature of his

---

* *Die Frage an den Einzelnen*, p. 197; p. 66.
† *Ich und Du*, p. 24; p. 12.

thinking: he sees the remedy of the human predicament in the fulfilment of the relationship between the I and Thou.* Because of his quest for a remedy for "the sickness of time," he reaches a point where ontology is replaced by prescription.

---

* See the present author's *Spirit and Man* (The Hague: Nijhoff, 1963), pp. 20, 44 ff.

Chapter Eight

The Encounter

[1]

It is often assumed that if people, those who oppose one another, meet, their very meeting creates a new reality, which is characterized by mutuality and by the exchange of views and ideas. The implication is that the encounter itself brings the parties closer, and that the belief or anticipation that accompanies the encounter acts — at least to some extent — as a harmonizing factor in human reality. This assumption is thought to apply to many modes of human contact, including those in the political realm.

This assumption, however formulated, is very likely the point of departure for Buber's observations on the position of dialogue in human reality. His various descriptions are aimed at presenting a profile of the sphere lodged *between* human partners. In addition, he explicates several components of that sphere to make us aware of what is actually present in the human encounter as a dialogue (*Zwiesprache*) or from the position of the partners (*I* and *Thou*) embraced by that sphere of "between". Buber attempts further to make us aware not only of the presence of that sphere but also of the element of certainty that pervades it. For him that aspect of certainty is the basis of the description or analysis of the belief inherent in the interhuman situation. It can also be the basis for the phenomenon of faith in the trans-human sense — that is to say, in the sense of the relationship between the human being and God. This belief is the human being's conviction that the encounter has a certain content, namely that each partner in the relationship has its own reality. Signifying the encounter between present beings, dialogue is thus the hard core (and *coeur*) of the atmosphere surrounding human beings in their mutual encounters and in their presence in the world. In Buber's view, dialogue is not only descriptive of a central mode of human co-existence, it is also posited as an educational and moral idea for guiding human existence both within the interhuman sphere and within the sphere that exists between the human being and God. Thus for Buber, as we have seen, the sphere of "between" is both a basic fact of human reality and the central norm of behavior grounded in that reality.

Buber not only described the position of the dialogue in the interhuman context, he appealed to it, believing that the appeal was powerful enough to anchor the educational consequences of dialogue. An indication of the extent to which Buber took encounter not only as infrastructure and norm, but also as a therapeutic device for the labyrinth of human problems is a conversation between himself and the great physicist Niels Bohr that took place in Jerusalem at the height of the cold war. Buber presented the view, to which Bohr responded with scepticism, that the very meeting between the representatives of the superpowers would gradually lead to mitigation of the cold war. That is to say, Buber understood dialogue as a creative factor in reality even on the international, collective level.

[2]

Replying to comments by Walter Kaufmann, Buber said: "The nature, strictly speaking, of my thought to traditional philosophy seems to me more a theme for my critics than for me."* But regardless of Buber's reluctance to refer to philosophical arguments inherent in the philosophical tradition, and apart from the everyday aspect of dialogue, three philosophical motifs can be discerned behind his reflections on dialogue. The first can be described as the search for certainty in our propositions and statements. That certainty does not refer to the self-enclosed I or ego, in the sense of "I think, therefore I am," which emphasizes the position of the I. The philosophical quest here is for a certainty which, from the very beginning, breaks open that self-enclosedness by primary reference to the Thou in the sense formulated

---

* We refer here to *Philosophical Interrogations*, edited, with an introduction, by Sydney and Beatrice Rome (New York, Chicago, San Francisco: Holt, Rhinehart and Winston, 1964). The interrogation of Martin Buber, conducted by Maurice S. Friedman, appears on pp. 13 ff, the comment quoted above on p. 17.

by Friedrich Heinrich Jacobi: "Thou exist and I exist." The referential or comprehensive character of the certainty of existence could not be understood as a consequence of an argument, demonstration, or syllogism. It was conceived in the first place as "immediate certainty", which can be understood as certainty grounded in the actual and direct contact or relation between human beings. It does not presuppose an introspection secluded within a state of mind, except that which is inherent in mutual recognition. The philosophers of immediacy assert this mutual immediate certainty rather than the reflective certainty of Descartes.* This immediacy or directness needs to be analyzed more specifically and concretely.

Here a second point of philosophical reasoning arises, if such can be spoken of in the context of a philosophy of immediacy. There is the well-known problem of the mode of knowing whether what is present before the ego is an object in mind or an alter ego, a Thou. This problem poses additional questions as to the very adequacy of a mode of cognition that uses analytical tools, to establish that an object present before the I has certain features, a head, eyes, etc. But how can the I sum up these particular features and be aware of their total *Gestalt*? How can the I justify its conclusion or awareness that this sum total authorizes it to conceive or perceive the present fragment of reality as a person and to behave as one would toward a Thou, not as one would toward an object? This question is related to a possible transition from general awareness of an object to the specific position of the Thou in its *Gestalt* as a being parallel to the I and combining existence and essence.

The dialogical conception characteristic of Buber and his philosophy of immediacy, which took shape as the dialogical principle, amounts to the position that the alter ego is revealed as a Thou in the very dialogue with him or her. Dialogue is to be understood not only as a mode of linguistic communication, but also as a broad interhuman context, which is both the basis of human mutuality and its central shaping factor. There is no first step in that mutuality. I talk to the Thou because he is a Thou and the Thou is posited in that status

---

* Buber's relation to the philosophy of immediacy can probably be traced to his teacher Wilhelm Dilthey; see, for instance Dilthey's *Beiträge zur Lösung der Frage vom Ursprung unseres Glauben an die Realität der Aussenwelt*, 1890 (cited earlier). On this see: I.Berlin, "Hume and the Sources of German Anti-Rationalism," in *David Hume* (Edinburgh: Edinburgh University Press, 1977, pp. 93 ff.) See also the present author's: "On Nihilism — Hamilton's Contribution," *Archiv für Geschichte d. Phil.*, 1980 (62), pp. 46ff. Consult: Arthur O. Lovejoy, *The Reason, the Understanding and Time* (Baltimore: The Johns Hopkins Press, 1961).

because I am talking to him or her. Dialogue inheres in the status of the I and the Thou, but also constitutes that status. Or, to put it the other way around, the I and the Thou constitute the *Zwiesprache*, but the *Zwiesprache* in turn constitutes the I and the Thou. Dialogue is a kind of dynamic medium, while the I and the Thou are the partners engaged in the dynamic process of the medium. Furthermore, dialogue is imbued with faith or certainty that requires no demonstration or proof.

The third point to be made in our attempt to understand the philosophical background of the philosophy of immediacy and dialogue is actually an amplification of the second point. We are not concerned with cognition within the inter-human reality as such, but with the features that enable us to distinguish between illusion and reality, between dream and fact, between what we encounter and what we imaginatively produce, etc. Here the philosophy of immediacy presents an appeal to what Hume called belief — and which, together with some of the deliberations underlying its formulation, was taken over by Jacobi. The reasoning can be summed up as follows: even when it is difficult or impossible to verify our opinion that something really exists, the reality of the Thou penetrates not only one's self-enclosedness but also the alleged circle of dreams in which one may be immersed. The Thou exists, and his or her existence is no less certain than one's own. In spite of the fact that the context of relations between oneself and the Thou lacks a corporeal realization, and perhaps even a sensuous manifestation, it is the context of reality. Dialogue is thus a manifestation of a reality and can be understood as pointing directly, or immediately, to the reality surrounding human beings.

Buber was influenced by these three motifs and incorporated them in the structure of his own thinking, giving them expression in his many writings. He emphasized the immediacy of the relationship between one human being and another. Furthermore, he tried to show that this immediacy could be a point of departure for a description of a religious experience, because that experience is characterized by an attitude and not by an article of faith, by listening and not by a formula, let alone a dogma.

To be sure, the dialogical attitude has a broader scope than dialogue in the linguistic sense, which is an utterance of sounds or production of gestures. Language may be soundless and still be expressive of understanding and response between human beings or of their dynamic co-presence. Thus, Buber's main interest in dialogue is not as a communication that has language as its medium (even though he called one of his major works *Zwiesprache*) — but as a mode of existence and comprehensive human reality. Dialogue, or conversation, is an expression in two senses: expression in terms of language, but also the manifestation crystallized in language of the broad infrastructure of interhuman relations.

[3]

Buber says of himself that he describes the conduct of life. He presents things as they are, and does not demand anything nor is he entitled to do so. He claims to be accepting the world. In contrast to dialectic, the life of dialogue is no privilege of spirituality. Here there are no gifted and ungifted, but only those who give themselves and those who withhold themselves. Dialogue is not an affair of spiritual luxury; it is matter of man as a creature. Buber apparently thought that the very fact that he gave prominence to this structure of human reality paved the way for human behaviour in the normative sense, since wherever man hears a voice and responds to it, he by the same token also shapes the conduct of existence. We can say, therefore, that explicit normative rules are less important than the intrinsic implications of response, and that the world or normative order is shaped more by the latter than by the former. Our very acceptance of the world is itself an act in that world. This is so because the most adequate response to that acceptance is the attitude of care for what is entrusted to me, and the expression of that attitude is to help the world in the process of its maturation: I do not think about changes, but only that the world I have received should continue to exist and mature. This attitude is the human response to what Buber takes to be a basic fact, namely that the world entrusted to me has to be accompanied by my own trust or loyalty. Here trust and responsiveness coincide. This in fact brings us back to the issue of the relation between the given basis of human existence and the imperative to shape it.

Buber attempts to derive norms related to human behavior from the primary fact that the human being dwells in the world and responds to it. That, as was discussed earlier, is the basis for his deliberations concerning responsibility, in the literal sense of the term, *qua Verantwortung*. Genuine responsibility exists only where there is real responding. Buber's aphorisms are permeated by associations and word play as well as by an attempt to look into the primary etymological meaning of terms, and it is obvious that here he takes advantage of the affinity between responding *qua antworten* and responsibility *qua Verantwortung*. It might be noted that Hebrew word play, for instance, does not lead in that particular direction, because the Hebrew term meaning "responsibility", *ahrayut*, suggests a standing behind, not a responding. Be that as it may, Buber attempts to show that care is a correlate of responding, and the latter is an attitude of listening and answering. The linguistic aspect of voicing and hearing is thus both a model for describing the conduct of life and a crystallization of care and involvement in the circle of reality within which the human being exists.

It is in this context of the meaning of response that Buber also points to the primacy — and superiority — of religion over morality. The crux of morality is in its being a postulate, while religion, as he says, has the advantage over morality in that it is a phenomenon and not a postulate. That is to say, religion is essentially an attitude towards comprehensive reality, while morality is basically a formulation of imperatives. In this sense morality is, by definition, a sum-total of acts of intervention in the course of reality, and, as we have seen, intervention is a shift away from the primary attitude of acceptance of the world at large and of the particular realm of human reality. Religion is closer to the attitude of response, while morality is by definition an attitude of shaping. What is more, religion covers a broader field than morality. Morality is essentially related to demands, and hence to the demanding agent, and therefore also has a place in religion; religion, however does not have a place in morality. One may wonder, of course, whether at this point Buber had in mind Kant's philosophy of religion, namely that morality as such stands in no need of a religious grounding, and religion appears — if at all — as supplementary to morality. These points have to be emphasized, because they again bring into relief the programmatic attempt to describe and to report, and if possible to find in the described reality the anchor for an "ought". For Buber the concept of responsibility is to be brought back from the province of specialized ethics, where an "ought" hovers freely in the air over lived life.

[4]

A closer analysis of the phenomenon of responsibility will enable us to consider the inescapable critical question of whether or not Buber's descriptions can be taken as an adequate and comprehensive report of human existence. This analysis will lead us once again to the aspects of thinking and reflection and their impact, even though they are not immersed in immediacy.

When Buber points to responsibility as related to response, he does not bring into prominence what might be described metaphorically as the burden of responsibility, nor does he point to the phenomenon of seeking responsibility, since he emphasizes, even over-emphasizes, the given reality and the response to it. Yet, a person does not only respond to another person, but also decides to be responsible or open to another person. We may mention at this juncture the four situations of responsibility distinguished by Roman Ingarden: a person bears responsibility for something; takes responsibility for something; is held responsible; acts responsibly. The decision inherent in the situation of taking responsibility upon oneself or acting responsibly is not only a decision vis-a-vis another person but also vis-a-vis a certain cause or value like health, education, homeland, etc. In addition, behind responsibility and the responsive attitude lies what Ingarden calls the ontic basis of responsibility, namely the identity of the acting person. That is to say, the person is not only involved in the I-Thou relationship but is also a person in the sense of being self-enclosed and as such is both a deciding agent and a responsive being.* Because Buber tends to identify responsibility with responsiveness, he disregards the notion or phenomenon of the responding person who is a single, acting individual, though being single does not necessarily imply solitariness or detachment from the interpersonal situation. A person can still be involved in dialogues while being, at the same time, a pre-dialogical entity and a trans-dialogical one. These various dimensions of his existence enrich the dialogue and are enriched by it.

Remaining with the German expressions, we may say that the over-emphasis on response led to a belittling of the component of *Zurechnung* (accountability), which is also an element in the phenome-

---

* Roman Ingarden, *Über die Verantwortung, ihre ontischen Fundamente*, (Stuttgart: Philipp Reclam Jun., 1970), pp. 5, 58. See also the present author's analysis of responsibility in his *Theory and Practice, An Essay on Human Intentionalities* (The Hague: Martinus Nijhoff, 1977), pp. 184 ff.

non of responsibility. Accountability implies the attribution to an agent of acts, as well as moods and attitudes which are neither tangible nor visible. In all these components the ontic position of the agent is manifest, and as we have said an agent is not only a partner in an I-Thou relationship. That is to say, dialogue cannot obliterate the self-referring and self-reflecting person's awareness of himself. This issue, we may observe, keeps returning in different contexts.

This last observation draws attention once again to the component of self-awareness and reflection. Reflection is the condition for attributing acts to an agent. It is also the medium through which the ontic position of the agent is affirmed by that very attribution. With this in mind, we may consider the following statement: "... the consciousness of the I-Thou relation is a highly intensive one; but it is a direct, an elementary consciousness. It does not make itself an object; it does not detach itself from itself; its knowing about itself is given it with its being."[*] But the fact that a mode of consciousness is intensive does not necessarily make it direct or elementary. When such a consciousness is not our object, that is to say when we do not reflect upon it, this is certainly an outcome of our own decision. We may say that it is a reflection that erases itself by our decision not to reflect. Furthermore, its knowing is not given with its being, and we must distinguish between consciousness as such and particular active attentiveness directed at a specific situation.

Buber says that Socrates overvalued the significance of abstract general concepts as compared to concrete individual experiences.[†] In stating that, he posits a dichotomy between general and individual concepts that cannot be maintained since even the act of identification performed by an individual uses concepts. For instance, in identifying an individual we identify him or her as a human being and his or her individual character or presence is in a way a *differentia specifica*. We focus on the individual, but we presuppose the general. In this sense we cannot escape reflection, consciousness and knowing — which are not just inherent in being, as Buber suggested.

Consciousness is not totaly congruent with linguistic communication, and we cannot escape the problem of the relationship between thinking and language. Buber mentions Wilhelm von Humboldt, but not his view of the inner relationship between thinking and language. Humboldt described reflection, metaphorically, as the pause of the

---

[*] *Interrogations*, p. 39.
[†] Ibid., pp. 47, 67.

mind vis-a-vis impressions.* Buber speaks of turning the thinking dialectic into a dialogue, and asks: when will the action of thinking bear, include and mean the presence of the opposite experiencing being? But it is clearly not enough to refer to thinking in this way. Buber says that "reflecting" as *Zuruckstrahlen* — lightening back — points to the fact that even in the primary stage of the act of thinking we refer to a genuine Thou and not only to an internal one. But in this context we have to ask whether a person is recognized immediately, directly, as an experiencing being or whether that recognition is an interpretation of our experience? Is it not an interpretation of our *Erfahrung* that leaves us with the cognition, or recognition, that the being before us is engaged in an *Erlebnis* of his or her own? (The English: "experience" connotes both *Erfahrung* and *Erlebnis*)

We cannot escape the conclusion, or let us say the reflection, that Buber attempts to characterize the encounter directly, that is to say, immediately, as if the characterization were itself a part of the described situation. He says that existence is not one philosophical theme among others. "Here witness is made". Disregarding the question of who is bearing witness, and staying with the situation of bearing witness, we have to ask ourselves whether the witness is warranted or corroborated. The very fact that I give evidence is not itself evidence in the philosophical sense, that is to say, it is not a statement that offers certainty. Buber says that he welcomes every philosophy of existence that leaves the door open leading to otherness. He adds a qualification which, in a sense, refers to his own philosophy as well, namely that he does not know anyone who opens the door wide enough. But even when we adopt that metaphor, we still face the problem of evaluating both the openness and the door. Just to point to them is not enough.

[5]

Behind language lies the creativity of the mind or of the spirit, what Humboldt described as *energeia*. *Energeia* cannot be fully integrated into the fabric of human relations in terms of responsiveness; thinking is not only reflection and reproduction but also production. As such

---

* See Humboldt's programmatic text and its analysis in the present author's: "Humboldt's Prolegomena to Philosophy of Language", *Cultural Hermeneutics*, 1974, pp. 211 ff.

it is manifested in the creation of concepts, the establishment of relations among them and of propositions based upon them, the drawing of conclusions, weighing of arguments, entertaining of intentions and plans in the creation of ideas and representations, and the maintaining of consciousness of all this — all in all, what is called the exploration of the truth by way of discourse. That discursive quality is lacking, and not by accident, in the philosophy of immediacy and in Buber's version of it.* To be sure, his philosophy of immediacy is one of responsiveness and not just one of giving expression to the self — here lies the specific quality of his philosophy but also its vulnerability. A comment to be taken up presently will throw additional light on that aspect of Buber's philosophy. It is made by Georg Simmel, who influenced Buber,† and is related to the description and analysis of the social situation

[6]

> By 'meeting' in the pregnant sense in which I use the word, I understand an occurence of the genuine I-Thou relation, in which the one partner affirms and confirms the other as this unique person. That the lines of these relations intersect in the eternal Thou is grounded in the fact that the man who says Thou ultimately means his eternal Thou.‡

In spite of the significance of the issue, in the present context we do not have to go into the question of how we can distinguish between the human Thou and the eternal Thou. We confine ourselves instead to the awareness of the Thou as inherent in our meeting it, which is obviously the central point in Buber's philosophy. It is at this point that we refer to Simmel, who suggests a distinction between knowing within the interhuman relationship and being aware of what we know or deliberately referring to knowledge. He says that it is amazing how much we know in our everyday behaviour and contact with human beings. What we know are general characteristics, that is to say, features which one being shares with others. We grasp those features immediately while referring to the individuality of the part-

---

* See: Yochanan Bloch, *Die Aporie des Du, Probleme der Dialogik Martin Bubers* (Heidelberg: Verlag Lambert Schneider, 1977), pp. 222, 84, 105, et passim.
† G. Scholem remarks that Buber was a disciple and great admirer of Simmel; Gershom Scholem, *Von Berlin nach Jerusalem*, (Frankfurt: Bibliothek Suhrkamp, 1977), p. 89.
‡ *Interrogations*, p. 114.

ner, whose very appearance tells us something about him.* The point is that even what is described as immediate contact is not merely an awareness of the presence of the other. Along with and inseparable from that is an awareness of qualities, and thus an act of recognition in the basic sense of that term. We come to know the present partner and we recognize, that is cognize again, features of which we were aware in the first place. For us the immediate contact is not a realization of an amorphous position, since we reflect and through reflection are aware of qualities whether or not we articulate that awareness. Existence and essence are analytically different, even on the level of interpersonal contact. It seems that Buber tried to read the interhuman situation, as it were, from within and did not reflect programmatically and factually on the fact that — to come back to the metaphor — when one reads, even from within, he still *reads* the situation he intentionally refers to.

Striving for immediacy, Buber saw it as self-enclosed and did not present a horizon on which the I-Thou is to be lodged — and we may add, objectively. But the objective perspective is legitimate not only for orientation but also for understanding, since, as Simmel observed, society is an intermediate structure between the subject and the non-personal generality and objectivity.† These and cognate aspects are absent in Buber's version of immediacy. This is also the point to be made in terms of the built-in difference between dialogue and dialectic.

---

* Georg Simmel, *Soziologie, Untersuchungen uber die Formen der Vergesellschaftung*, 2. Aufl. (München und Leipzig: Verlag von Dunker und Humblot, 1922), p. 485.
† Ibid., p. 152. See: Emmanuel Levinas, "Martin Buber and the Theory of Knowledge," in *The Philosophy of Martin Buber*, edited by Paul Arthur Schilpp and Maurice Friedman, The Library of Living Philosophers, vol. XII, Open Court, Lassalle, Cambridge University Press, London, 1967, pp. 133ff. Buber replied to the points raised in the same volume, pp. 695ff.

Chapter Nine

Immediacy or Mediation?

[1]

Dialogue obviously has a linguistic connotation — in terms, of course, of "parole" and not "langue". Buber, however, removes dialogue from the confines of the delimited linguistic mode and posits it as epitomizing a mode of existence — *Zwiesprache* becomes *Zwischen* — In Between. Let us examine this through a juxtaposition of the dialogical interpretation of existence and the inner logic of dialectic.

Buber's basic approach to human existence can be characterized by two interrelated points: a) the core of human existence lies in the interpersonal relation between one human being and another, and b) that relation is immediate not only in terms of expression but also in terms of philosophical identification, as was explained earlier. In this view, the alleged immediate interpersonal encounter of the *I-Thou* relation is sufficient for identification. That identification as *Gestalt* need not be preceded by philosophical articulation. The self-sufficiency of immediacy is apparently warranted by the fact that we are aware of immediate interpersonal relations since we realize them in our day-to-day behavior. It therefore seems unnecessary to analyze that pattern of relations. Such analysis necessarily leads to mediation (*Vermittlung*), and thereby to the introduction of dialectical concept.

A juxtaposition of Buber's dialogic with Hegel's dialectic can help to shed light on this structural aspect of Buber's thought. To be sure, references to Hegel are infrequent in Buber's writings although, as he once said, he did study Hegel's *Phenomenology* in a seminar with Dilthey, including the chapter on the master and the servant. Furthermore, there is an explicit, though short, presentation of Hegel's conception of man in Buber's *Das Problem des Menschen*. We shall therefore begin by considering the main points of that presentation.

[2]

Buber starts off by characterizing Hegel's system and its influence as dispossessing (*Depossedierung*) the concrete human person.[*] The implication is that man is fundamentally present but has been deposed by the system. Buber's presentation of Hegel amplifies this polemical characterization.

Buber observes that unlike the young Hegel, the systematic philosopher Hegel did not start from man but from *Weltvernunft*,[†] — Reason of the world — thus suggesting that there exists a contradiction between reason, its cause and manifestation in the world, and the concrete position of human beings. Accordingly, he characterizes Hegel's system, following St. Thomas', as the logological attempt.[‡] The duplication of "logos" is meant to indicate the shift from concrete reality, which is encountered and not thought of, to an overriding comprehensive structure focussed on reason. One aspect of that shift from concreteness to reason is the fact that solitude is overcome and the question about man is obliterated (*ausgetilgt*).[§] It is clear, then, that there is an inner relationship between concreteness and solitude, and in turn between the two and the very position of the human being. If this is the case, than the interpersonal *I-Thou* attitude may itself include solitude in spite of the dialogical position as an embracing sphere between human beings. The I within the I-Thou relation does not cease to be an I - nor is it immersed in a world-spirit (*Weltgeist*) or logos. Solitude emphasizes the status of the I as constantly present. The attempt here seems to be aimed at preserving both the I and the I-Thou, or the I within the sphere of relation.

The abolition — or sublation — of concreteness is made prominent in Hegel's system, according to Buber, in terms of the position of time. Buber counterposes the concrete time of human beings and what he describes as time thought of (*gedankliche Zeit*). The latter is also the cosmological time, or time in the comprehensive sense, which is the

---

[*] *Das Problem des Menschen*, ibid., p. 348; p. 170.
[†] Ibid., p. 350; p. 138.
[‡] Ibid., p. 351; p. 139.
[§] Ibid., p. 352; p. 140.

same as the time of the logos. It goes without saying that Buber does not go into the many aspects and problems of Hegel's system at this juncture.

There is another aspect in Buber's short presentation of Hegel that has a bearing on both the philosophy of I-Thou and Buber's philosophy of faith or religion. He emphasizes that the element of trust cannot be transferred to the structure of Hegel's system. In Hegel, as summarized by Buber, faith in creation is replaced by a conviction about development, faith in revelation by a conviction about increasing knowledge, while faith in salvation is transformed into a conviction about the perfection of the world. But, adds Buber, only trust in that which merits trust can establish a relation of unconditioned certainty toward the future.*

It seems to be warranted to assume that trust is taken as an irreducible attitude grounded in the relation inherent in the interpersonal sphere but also beyond that, where the Thou connotes the divinity. Trust cannot be replaced by any equivalent in the cosmological structure of the world, since trust is an attitude and not a structure. Buber probably wanted to assert that structures can be replaced, as for instance, the structure of a process can be replaced by a dialectical articulation of it. Attitudes cannot be replaced; they are immediate manifestations and — this is an explication of Buber's view — no articulation can replace immediacy since any such replacement is itself a shift from what is given concretely to what ceases to be concrete by that very shift. Concreteness is immediately encountered and no conceptual statement can be adequate vis-a-vis it. That which is immediately given can, however, be adequately grasped only by an immediate awareness of it.

[3]

Having said this, it might be appropriate to give some attention to Hegel's analysis of the relation between master and servant. That relation is Hegel's point of departure for establishing the symmetry of the two, thus overcoming the initial preponderance of the master over the servant. We ask whether Buber's summary of Hegel's position does justice to the complicated aspects of dialectic and hence —

---

* Ibid., p. 356; p. 142.

by the same token — to the allegedly unbridgeable contradiction between immediacy and mediation.

In the first place, Hegel's analysis of the relation between dominance and servitude is not an attempt to present the emergence of self-consciousness at the two poles of this relationship as a process in time. He attempts, rather, to discern the structure implicit in the relation between the master and the servant. He chooses that relationship as his point of departure since the master and servant are *prima facie* two poles of a structure between which there is a built-in lack of equilibrium. The discernment of self-consciousness by the parties at the two ends of the structure is meant to show that the explication of the relationship, accomplished through mediation, leads us to identify a symmetry not present at the imbalanced beginning.

Hegel points to the existence of the relation between dominance and servitude among the Greeks and Romans, emphasizing that historically the two peoples did not elevate themselves to the concept of absolute freedom. He probably wanted to emphasize that there is a built-in connection between the symmetry between the master and his servant and the presence of freedom. The reference to historical peoples is meant to call our attention to the fact that the discernment of factors in the relation has a historical dimension but is not essentially or exclusively an historical phenomenon. The concrete historical dimension itself has a structural character.

With respect to the structure, Hegel says that the serving person is selfless (*selbstlos*) and vis-a-vis his own self has another self i.e. the master. The will of the serving person dissolves in his fear of the master (*in der Furcht des Herrn*).[*] There is an inner relation between fear and serving but, dialectically, the very need of the master to take advantage of the services of the being he confronts and uses leads to his acknowledgment of the servant. From the vantage of the master the servant's instrumentality brings about recognition of him not only in his instrumental position but also as a creature endowed with self-consciousness and thus as a human being. The emphasis in Hegel is on the aspect of acknowledgment or recognition (*Anerkennung*),[†] though the acknowledgment becomes present through the mediation of the attitude of taking advantage of the servant, and as such is not a manifestation of equality. What is presently or immediately given

---

[*] *Phil. Propädeutik*, Glockner's Ausgabe, vol. III (Stuttgart: Fromann Verlag,) pp. 110f.

[†] *Phänomenologie des Geistes*, Glockner's Ausgabe, vol. II, p. 154.

is the instrumental position of the servant. But that very position contains the next step beyond itself leading toward acknowledgment and the emergence of self-consciousness.

It is not necessary here to go into further details of Hegel's analysis.[*] The hard core is Hegel's attempt to analyse structural aspects of an interhuman relation that begins with a lack of symmetry and eventually emerges as a symmetrical relation. Again, one could say that an historical process is present in that "development". But what is essential is not the temporal aspect but the structural embracement of immediacy as a lack of symmetry and a mediated position that is imbued with symmetry. The historical process can be seen, to put it in Kantian terms, as a schema of the mediated relationship but the schema is not the structure as such. We shall see once again that the aspect of immediacy versus mediation is central for Buber's position — and here immediacy is meant to connote not just one component but the full *Gestalt*.

[4]

Buber uses the term "spirit", which is a fundamental term in Hegel's system though not confined to it. Here are some of Buber's remarks on the subject. It is said that spirit is not within the I but between the I and the Thou.[†]

The assertion that the essence of spirit is to mature to the situation of being able to say Thou[‡] is probably a variation of the previous statement, though if we read the text closely we are bound to notice that this characterization contains an element of possibility or potentiality implied in becoming mature. In this sense spirit does not connote the relation between the I and Thou as such but — or perhaps also the potentiality of that relation. As a potentiality, spirit would connote something inherent within each of the partners and not the given or present relation between them, because that relation is more an actuality than a potentiality.

This hesitation concerning the position of spirit is reinforced by the statement that language is the primary act of the spirit. It is stated

---

[*] See the analysis in the present author's, *Legislation and Exposition, Critical Analysis of Differences between the Philosophy of Kant and Hegel*, Hegel-Studien, Beiheft 15 (Bonn: Bouvier Verlag Herbert Grundmann), 1984, pp. 37 ff.
[†] *Ich und Du*, p. 49; p. 39.
[‡] Ibid., p. 103; p. 95.

further that the word exists in eternity.* We may wonder what this actually means. What, first of all, is the relation between spirit and language? As a primary act, language cannot be a potentiality because an act, not only etymologically, is an actuality. Further still: in what sense can we speak of eternity in the context of the I-Thou relation, since eternity is a position beyond self-contained relations? It could perhaps be suggested that the relation between language and spirit refers to spirit in a comprehensive sense, whereas Buber confines spirit to its manifestation in the relation between human beings. This suggestion receives reinforcement from Buber's statement that the world of the Thou has no connection with space or time.† Again we may wonder whether this lack of connection is an indication of the aspect of eternity — at least some sense of it — or whether it points to a kind of abstraction that occurs within the relation between the I and the Thou.

It should be mentioned here that Buber refers to the a priori of relation,‡ and we are bound to ask what this means in this context. If the I-Thou relation is an irreducible whole, how is the component of a priori brought into this context, for a priori connotes something that can be isolated from the context and be self contained. Is the a priori the very relation and its structure? If so, Buber would be introducing a formal aspect into his presentation — and we may wonder whether this would be congruent with the trend of his thinking. Our doubt is strengthened by his statement that in the beginning there was relation.§ We are unclear as to what extent the a priori, which has a functional meaning, coincides with "the beginning," which has a temporal meaning. Be that as it may, the use of formal or structural descriptions does not suit the trend and mode of knowledge or acquaintance related to the I and Thou. Presumably Buber speaks of the a priori and of the beginning as immediate in order to point to the lack of conceptuality and even of what is called pre-knowledge (*Vorwissen*). The encounter itself is all of real life.

On the one hand Buber characterizes the I-Thou relation as a priori, thus attributing a formal position to it. On the other hand he attempts to endow it with the meaning of holiness, giving it a position which, to say the least, cannot be formal. Indeed, in describing relation he speaks of the sanctity of the primary word (*im heiligen Grundwort*).¶

---

*   Ibid., p. 108; p. 100.
†   Ibid., p. 79; p. 69.
‡   Ibid., p. 30; p. 18.
§   Ibid., p. 21; p. 9.

This again is an amplification of the basic position of the I-Thou relation. That relation is fundamental to such an extent and depth that it is endowed with the quality of being holy. Holiness here probably implies not a separated position (though Buber alludes to Rudolf Otto) but the position of being fundamental. It is not separated because the relation between the human being and God is also a relation between I and Thou. The sacred quality of that relation is transferred, as it were, to the I-Thou relation between one human being and another. We dealt earlier with the issue as to which level of the I-Thou relation — the interhuman or that between the human being and God — is primary.

[5]

A brief examination of the meaning of the concept of spirit in Hegel's system will enable us to highlight some problematic aspects of Buber's employment of that concept. In the first place, in Hegel spirit connotes the comprehensive reality that asserts itself. Hence, one of the qualities of spirit is true infinity (*die wahrhafte Unendlichkeit*).[*] Infinity is not given, it develops, and its development is both the explication of spirit and the process leading towards its realization. In this sense the two aspects of spirit — knowledge (or self-knowledge) and freedom — are correlated. Knowledge is inherent in spirit because one of the explications of comprehensiveness is that the comprehensive reality is a reality that knows itself. Freedom is inherent in spirit because freedom is a self-assertion that posits something out of its own resources. The articulation or development of spirit is by the same token a development within spirit and thus - from this angle too - is to be described as freedom. For Hegel the conjunction of knowledge and will is a step in the direction of bringing together the theoretical and practical aspects of spirit. It is an additional attempt — problematic as it is — to reinforce the comprehensive aspect of spirit. Eventually, that comprehensiveness is focussed in the description of spirit as subject sublating (*aufhebend*) substance. From the systematic and methodical point of view, it has to be said that in this sense spiritual reality is given but is also potentiality; that is so

---

¶ Martin Buber, *Two Types of Faith*, trans. Norman P. Goldhawk (New York: Harper & Brothers, 1961), p. 9.
* Ibid., p. 29.

because the actuality of spiritual reality is related to the process of self-explication and thus to mediation i.e. substance becoming subject. Subject is both comprehensive and knowing itself.

In Buber's presentation, spirit is not comprehensive in the sense of being the total reality. It is the relation between I and Thou, an immediately given and present. It is thus confined to the interhuman sphere. Accordingly, there exist only sporadic "islands" of relation that depend on the experiencing of the relation by the I and the Thou. Furthermore, because these relations are expressed in terms of "witness", they cannot be assessed by an outside observer nor be subjected to theoretical articulation or analysis. The partners in the relation assert themselves, and the sphere comprising the "whole" of the partners and their mutuality is identified as spirit.

Here we come upon a fundamental problem related to Buber's theory but which also has a broader bearing. The question is to what extent a philosophical approach — as opposed to a literary expression — can be confined to assertions that formulate experiences without attempting to analyse those assertions in terms of their conceptual components. The relation between the I and Thou presents that problem in a very pointed way. The I-Thou relation is sporadic rather than continuous; one encounter between the I and Thou may carry within itself the traces of previous encounters even though the Thou in the relationship may be a different person. Furthermore, the I-It relationship is present within the horizon of the specific I-Thou mutuality and thus there is no escape from the awareness — i.e., reflection — of the distinction between I-Thou and I-It. Is the distinction only a passive framework or does it have a bearing on the actual relationship between the I and Thou? Moreover, we cannot ignore the fact that I-Thou as a structural relation is a generality. The very position of the Thou as a non-It, or even anti-It, is already a conceptual position by way of comparison or exclusion, explicit or not. As such, it is only a point of departure for more specific aspects of the relationship brought under the common heading of I-Thou. Concretely they differ from one another and may even be mutually opposed. Hence, I-Thou is a structure and cannot be identical with an immediate experience here and now.

As a matter of fact, this is a fundamental shortcoming in any philosophical approach that not only starts with immediate data but attempts to remain within their sphere. Such an attempt consciously denies the need for explication, since an explication involves the position of an observer and a conceptual frame of reference that is beyond the experiential data inherent, for example, in the I-Thou relationship.

The problematic aspect of immediacy is made more prominent. When Buber enlarges the scope of his concern and identification of the immediate data and moves from the I-Thou in the inter-individual sense to the relation between the person and the national community. Once that step is taken, the question arises as to the relation between the interpersonal sphere and that of the I's involvement in a national or historical reality. Can that mode of relation be immediate or does it call for awareness of the transpersonal dimension of human existence?

Buber's version of the philosophy of immediacy is an attempt to point to experiences (*Erlebnisse*). These cannot be exhausted in being described as such. The very description calls for an exposition. Thus we come back to the question implied in Hegel's statement that the spirit in general is not immediate, since only natural things are immediate.[*] Consciousness is the activity that lifts awareness above what is given or experienced.

[6]

Hegel sums up the dialectical relationship between immediate and mediated (*vermittelt*) knowledge by saying that the assumption that there is immediate knowledge is an indication that we are not aware of mediation (*Vermittelheit*); but knowledge in fact is mediated.[†] This statement seems relevant for the systematic and critical exploration of Buber's position. In the first place, it has to be said again that though the various attitudes are presented as if they were immediately given, they are given in a context, mainly the I-Thou and the I-It. That context, which is not an external framework, contains what can be described as a delineation of one mode of relation versus the other, a comparison and juxtaposition of the two modes. Further still, a person who asserts what is immediately given is not only a "witness" but also a spectator, for it is in that status that the frame of reference containing delineation and comparison is formulated or is already present in mind. We identify the various modes of relation, and identification is reading of the implicit ingredients of the modes of relationship. Thus

---

[*] Ibid., p. 170.
[†] *Phil. d. Religion*, I. Glockner's Ausgabe, vol. XV, p. 175.

the very presentation of a state of affairs is already an explication of the implicit. Buber himself is interested in explication. Therefore he is bound to assume that the explication is not an imposition of an understanding of the modes of relations but a continuation and leap from what is implicit to what becomes explicit. Thus, we come back to Hegel's statement: we may not know that the immediate is mediated but it is.

To be sure, Buber's own later analysis of what he called *Urdistanz und Beziehung* points to a shift from immediacy to mediation — though he himself does not use these terms. In that presentation (first published in 1950) Buber speaks about a universal frame of reference, which he presents as a category of being. That frame of reference is man.* Only from the point of view of man can there be what he describes as that which is the independent opposite (*ein selbständiges Gegenüber*).† It is not by chance that Buber introduced into his analysis the distinction between the environing world close to man and the world at large, and thus alluded to the world as the broad, or even broadest, frame of reference. He hints at a unity which can be thought‡ — and again his use of the concept of unity and its presentness in the encounter is an indication that he is concerned not only with modes of relation but also with totality,§ at least in Kant's sense of the idea of the world. The reciprocity between setting at a distance and entering into a relationship¶ is an explication of the basic fact that relationship as such is grounded in a context broader than itself, namely distance. There is no escaping the need for a conceptual frame of reference.

Against the background of distance Buber describes the authentic conversation, and by the same token the actual fulfilment of the relation between human beings, as connoting what he calls "acceptance of otherness" (*Akzeptation der Anderheit*).** Both components, acceptance and otherness, call to mind the struggle for recognition stressed by Hegel in his analysis of the master-slave relation. The component of recognition should probably be maintained even if we do not take the next step in Hegel's system, from mutual recognition

---

* Ibid., p. 90.
† Ibid., p. 175.
‡ In the Lambert Schneider, edition Heidelberg 1978,) p. 9 containing an editorial appendix by Lothar Stiehm texts relevant for Buber's position as well as parts of philosophical discussions of his systematic view.
§ Urdistanz und Beziehung, vol. 1 p. 421; p. 61.
¶ Ibid., p. 423; p. 63.
** Ibid.

to comprehensive or total self-consciousness. But recognition, or in Buber's terminology, acceptance, underlies or is inherent in the I-Thou relationship. Acceptance need not be viewed in terms of a need for affirmation, which Buber presents as something which man as man needs.* Affirmation presupposes acceptance. It is a step in the direction of a positive attitude by one person vis-a-vis another, while acceptance is the other side of the presence of persons.

We should mention in this context that Buber suggests that the chaos stormily surrounding (*umwittered*) human reality† is not essential for the analysis of the relationship as such. We can even put the issue in broader terms by saying that because of the complicated structure of the relation between human beings, it cannot possibly be placed only, even normatively only, on the level of the I-Thou dialogue. At most, the dialogue and its components can be seen as a focus of the broader context of human relations and probably as a norm for human relations. But a norm — to put it in general terms — addresses itself to a given reality. That reality, ontologically and descriptively speaking, is not confined to the I-Thou relation, even when that relation is granted the position of a guiding norm.‡

We can sum up some of the problematic aspects of Buber's philosophy by pointing again to the distinction between the ontological, and thus factual, situation on the one hand and the normative imperative on the other. The tendency to stress immediacy as inherent in the I-Thou relation is to be understood as the result of a conjunction of ontological identification and a normative presentation of what ought to guide conduct in the scope of interhuman relations. We might say, in other words, that the *I-Thou* is a primary conjunction of the "is" (*Sein*) and the "ought" (*Sollen*). By introducing the concept of *Urdistanz*, Buber is led to reexamine that conjunction. The I-Thou can be a norm against the background of the broad framework of human existence. There is mutual reconfirmation from the point of view of immediacy and mediation and from the point of view of the position of the "is" and the "ought". The dialectic is there: *Urdistanz* is *Beziehung* and *Beziehung* implies *Distanz*, though not *Urdistanz*. The dialectic is present even if not deliberately or systematically explored. But an "immediate" dialectic is certainly a paradox and perhaps even a contradiction in terms.

---

*   Ibid., p. 424; p. 64.
†   Ibid., pp.422ff; 62 ff.
‡   Ibid., p. 423; p. 63.

[7]

Israel is characterized by Buber as a community of faith that took its birth as a nation or people. The nation or people in turn took its birth as a community of faith. It is not clear, nor is it explained, how the encounter between individual human beings leads to a people or nation. A people is not an immediate common ground of individuals, for as an inter-generational entity it is beyond the direct and present "between" of individuals. Further still, Buber speaks about two aspects of permanence of reciprocity — fidelity and trust. Both exist in the actual realm of relationship between two persons. Yet again it is not clear in what sense we can speak of permanence of reciprocity. Even when we assume that the I and the Thou are permanent partners, the factors safeguarding their permanece are not permanent. Permanence goes beyond the scope of immediacy, as for example in the attitude of friendship.

In addition, we are bound to ask whether fidelity, for example, is confined to the interpersonal "between" or whether it also refers to the relation between the individuals and the community — and especially when that community is one of faith. This issue becomes even more salient when Buber says: "The origin of the Jewish *emuna* is in the history of a nation, that of the Christian *pistis* in that of individuals."

History is a transpersonal realm. As such it cannot have the character of the I-Thou encounter. Nor can it be classified as an It, since it is a sum total of diachronic relations and by the same token a sum total of creations or manifestations of creativity. Like language, it is transpersonal, yet present as a potentiality in the scope of individuals who interpret it by drawing from it. It is not immediate, and certainly not immediately realized by individuals in the scope of their existence. Interpretation is essential in the relation between individuals and history. Hence even before dealing with categorial issues like distance and relation, Buber's presentation leads beyond immediacy and the atmosphere allegedly accompanying and inherent in it. To come back to Simmel; history is more man life.

It goes without saying that Buber's committment to the renaissance of the Jewish people is related to the historical and religious faith of the people. That faith places special emphasis on the Land of Israel and the people's relation to it. The relation to the land is a particular manifestation of the broad framework of relations and can hardly be understood within the *elan* of *Zwiesprache*. Application of the dialogical structure to it would be a sort of metaphor. Moreover, the attachment to the land is grounded in the past. The land is present because it is part of space, but the devotion to it is related to its past. The aspects of space and time are brought together, but the act of bringing them together cannot be an immediate encounter; furthermore, no past is immediately present. The land is given; its meaning not. Its meaning implies the direction of the present to the past and that direction cannot be a dialogue. We notice in a more general way that the complexity of the situations both on the level of mutuality as well as on the level of the relations between past and present implies the activities of consciousness. Hence neither of the two ends can be seen as given. The dialectical dynamics is inherent in those levels, whereas the dialogue is at the most only one aspect of that dynamics.

Chapter Ten

Faith and Reciprocity

[1]

Faith and religion occupy a prominent position in Buber's thought, both biographically and systematically. In our exploration of these topics against the background of the central issue of immediacy, we face a difficulty from the outset in that etymologically "religion" is probably related to a coming back. In other words, the concept implies a situation previously present which is, in a sense, continuously restituted. Faith implies an attitude of confidence or hope. Once that attitude is posited within the scope of religion it implies the relation between confidence and hope, and implies that which gives rise to or reinforces these. The hope is well-grounded in the divine essence as a responding and even benevolent entity. People hope that God will respond to them and their hope is based on confidence in the essence of God. Hence, both in religion and faith there is an inherent relationship between the attitude and the pole to which it refers. Systematically speaking, these attitudes are open to a phenomenological investigation in terms of acts of intentionality because those acts are fundamentally exhibited a structure of correlation. As to the religious attitude the main issue is whether the human being and God involved in a correlation are of equal status, or as Hermann Cohen observed, God is the "center of gravity" in that correlation.

[2]

The structure of correlation is not prominent in Buber's book, *Daniel,*[*] published in 1913, the first exposition of his interpretation of religion, which preceded the dialogical stage in the development of his thought. The emphasis in this book is on what in German philosophy is called *Erlebnis,* and rendered into English as "experience". Experience, however, is both *Erlebnis* and *Erfahrung.* The former connotes what is felt by the individual or is given in the synthesis between the stream of psychic process and its particular content, without articulation of the two poles present in the analysis of acts of intentionality. Experience as *Erfahrung* connotes the encounter with what is given or made present by going out of the stream of intra-psychic process to meet that which is outside the individual. Here, when using the term "experience", we will mean *Erlebnis.*

Though religion is conceptually a relation to an entity beyond the scope of the inner life of human beings, Buber says that God's realization in man is impossible. What is possible, at most, is an inner presence of experience.[†] In other words, the emphasis is not on the external aspect of the experience, which would be its correlate, but on the inner aspect. If this is so, religious feelings have a self-enclosed character, i.e., they are within the person itself and not within the scope of intentionality to an object beyond consciousness. The quasi-reflective character of experience, what Buber refers to as "to experience the experience,"[‡] leaves us wondering what kind of second-level experience it is, or whether a first-level experience is implied in that experience of experience. We wonder whether this is the case because as a reflective attitude the second level would be a cognitive attitude accompanied by experience but different from that of the "stream of experience." Now, if experience and intuition are brought together and considered to be coterminous — and one may wonder whether phenomenologically this is the case — and if intuition is inherently an experience of unity, then the implied unity prevents us from regarding the experience of experience as grounded in a reflective attitude. For it then would be grounded in intuition, and as Buber stresses, the intuiting person is not aware of object and subject, whereas the reflective attitude is fundamentally accompanied by a

---

[*] Daniel, *Gespräche von der Verwirklichung* vol. 1. pp. 9ff.
[†] Ibid., pp. 42 ff.
[‡] Ibid., p. 16.

distinction between subject and object. The totalistic view of experience is bound to give rise to the question as to the religious character or ingredient of that sort of experience.

One possible interpretation is that the experience is related to the unity or totality of the world, though the problem of stepping out into the world remains unexplored in this stage of Buber's thought. What is significant is that the unity is to be sought not outside the world but within it.* Hence, since the point of departure is in experience as an immanently given occurrence or attitude, the correlate, if at all, is the world in its immanent structure or totality. If that attitude prevails or is the norm, says Buber, all the contradictions and antinomies are made indifferent.† However, the relation between experience and the unity of the world, or even the very access to the world, is not made explicit in this presentation. The question about approaching the world figures again in the attempt to bring together experience and deeds aimed at realization, and indeed *Daniel* is subtitled "Talks about Realization" (*Verwirklichung*), as we noted in Chapter One.

[3]

"Out of our own deed comes the unity." That unity does not come from the world, but from the person who is the origin and agent of the deed. "The true unity cannot be found, it can only be accomplished through deeds."‡ We have to ask here whether a deed can realize the unity of the world. After all, since every deed is sporadic or piecemeal, its correlate cannot be the unity of the world even if we suppose that that is its aim. Be that as it may, Buber seems to think that experience is closer to the practical than to the cognitive attitude. That affinity derives from the fact that a deed emerges from the person, and thus is grounded in his inner world, while cognition is essentially directed towards what is given and does not accomplish, create, or shape things. Perhaps because of that affinity Buber speaks of the "unbroken force of realization."§ What is unbroken here is the fact that realization goes on continuously, and no single act exhausts it or its ongoing impact. Yet the continuous character of the acts does not remove them

---
* Ibid., p. 73.
† Ibid., p. 74.
‡ Ibid., p. 75.
§ Ibid., p. 28.

from the scope of the doer and his deeds by allegedly transforming them into one total act that realizes the unity of the world.

Buber states that God wants to be realized?* What does that mean? After saying this, he adds that there is no reality but through the human being, who realizes or materializes himself and all being.† Does that mean that God wants to be realized within the human scope or within human experiences? If so, that would be a realization not in the sense of the materialization of an essence but in the ordinary English meaning of the term, as becoming aware. A more plausible interpretation, however, would emphasize the correlation between the human being and God and not God's immersion within the scope of experience. Furthermore, what does the statement mean that there is no reality other than through human beings? Does it imply an idealistic interpretation of the relation between *esse* and *concipi*? But such an interpretation is restrained by the statement that the human being realizes himself and all being. That assertion suggests that if reality at large is dependent on human beings, the realization would be through cognition and not through deeds because cognition may have the totality as its object while deeds aim at realization within a more limited scope. One could even say that the very employment of the term being or reality (*Sein*) points to a correlate and not to something to be absorbed within the inner stream of experience.

The emphasis on acts of realization as akin to experience is brought to the fore from an additional angle. It is said that realization brings about and proclaims a situation while what is called orientation separates and distinguishes between the various aspects of that situation.‡

Reality is the highest price of life and the eternal birth of God, says Buber.§ It is rather difficult to decipher the meaning of this statement. Because of the relation between God and realization and because realization is a continuous process, the eternal and continuous birth of God is perhaps related to realization. That is to say, realization is continuously unity and continuously "gives birth to God." In any case, it can be said critically that the dichotomy of experience and realization on the one hand and orientation on the other, has an anti-behavioristic connotation: by rejecting orientation as merely a reaction to objects Buber stresses active involvement and initiative out

---

*   Ibid., p. 44.
†   Ibid; ibid.
‡   Ibid., p.29.
§   Ibid., p. 49.

of one's own resources qua experience, realization as a going out to shape what is encountered.

[4]

In *Daniel*, Buber employs the distinction between religiosity and religion. He says that religiosity is distorted and becomes religion and church once it starts "to orient itself." In this presentation religiosity is the inner life of experience, while religion, in contrast to inner life or the experienced relation between the human being and God — with all the due reservations about the position of God in that statement — is not only a dogmatic position but also an organizational structure. The assumption that religion is a distortion of the inner life gives rise, however, to a basic question: Is there any content or message to religiosity as such?[*] One may wonder whether phenomenologically even an extreme subjectivization of religiosity can accept a situation whereby it is totally a feeling, i.e. an experience, for how then does God enter the context? The question of the relation between the immanent and the transcendent is a constant feature of both religion and religiosity. Thus, the dichotomy between the two has, at the least, to be less sharply drawn.

As mentioned before, *Daniel* was written and published before Buber's formulation of the position of encounter. It is sometimes said that the I-and-Thou stage of his thought marks a new beginning and is not continuous with the previous stage. One may wonder whether this is, or could be, the case regarding any thinker. It would perhaps be better to say, in a Hegelian way, that the later stage sublates (*aufhebt*) the previous one but does not eradicate it. More specifically, the aspect of immediacy being so dominant in the I-and-Thou presentation, leads to the conclusion that the later stage cannot be unrelated to the previous one. We shall now look into this.

[5]

Realization figures centrally in Buber's essay "Der Heilige Weg". There the concept is focused on the essence of Judaism. That is significant, but from the systematic point of view should not be taken

---

[*] Ibid., p. 41.

as exhaustive. What the "spirit of realization" is remains an open question. Buber himself refers to "the truth as deed" (*Tat*).* A deed can be taken as the medium for realization, since there obviously is a relation between practical acts and the broad notion of realization as bringing about a certain state of affairs. Yet, when it is stated that the true place of realization is the community, and that the true community is that in which the divine is realized among human beings,† we cannot but wonder about the meaning of the divine as that which is to be realized. Or to put it differently, in the process of realization we are bound to distinguish between the locus of realization and the norm or content to be realized. The locus is the community or the network of connections among human beings. The reference is no longer to the world at large but to the human dimension within the world. Even if we assume that from the human point of view there is an attitude described as "the spirit of realization", it amounts to an openness to go out and bring about a state of affairs. But the normative aspect related to that realization is still unclear.

Since our present concern is with realization within the religious domain, we wonder what God is in Buber's presentation of the divinity "an elementary present substance".‡ Polemically, the emphasis on presence and on substance is directed against what Buber describes as the "Kantian idea". But if God is present as a substance within the human domain and His presence is elementary — i.e., given — we cannot but quesition the position of realization. Buber says that God is to be seen within things only as a kernel (*keimhaft*), but He has to be realized between things.§ This statement connotes a shift from potentiality to actuality, realization being the bridge between the two states of affairs. But what is the meaning of the statement that God is present in things, or is to be seen in them? Is that presence a kind of a pantheistic inherence or is it a manifestation of the divine realm in the human sphere or in that between various things? If there is a component of manifestation, how can the core or norm be to realize God in the sense of placing Him in reality? Can we overcome the position of things and human beings as a manifestation of the divine and concurrently overcome the distance implicit in manifestation between the level of day-to-day reality and the position

---

* Der Heilige Weg, Ein Wort an die Juden und an die Völker, *Literarische Anstalt* (Frankfurt am Main: Rutten & Loening, 1919), p. 23.
† Ibid., p. 16.
‡ Ibid., p. 14.
§ Ibid., p. 15.

of God? Even when the conceptual aspect of these statements is not clear they continue to echo the position of immediacy which is so overriding in Buber's thought. Against that immediacy we have to recall Goethe's statement: "The true is similar to God, it does not appear immediately. We are bound to guess it out of its manifestations".*

In actual fact, in Buber's own statements we do encounter some hesitancy regarding the immediacy of realization, and perhaps even discern an approach that is irreconcilable with immediacy. Buber refers to "Mosaic legislation",† which by being a system of laws, implies distance between the system and the day-to-day reality in which realization is to take place. Divine legislation like the Mosaic code is a call that must first be understood and as such cannot be immediately grasped and immediately promote behaviour according to its norms, i.e., the prescriptions to guide the behaviour of realization.

Referring again to ancient Judaism, Buber speaks about the realization of the divine in natural life, or negatively that the direction to be followed is not one of remaining within the sphere of "pure spirit".‡ The dichotomy between pure spirit and natural life again raises the question as to the position of the divine element: does it belong to the sphere of pure spirit or to that of life, or is it an in-between sphere with an affinity to spirit yet directed toward the day-to-day reality referred to as life? There is a distinction between truth and reality, idea and fact, morality and politics,§ and we may wonder again whether the distinction or duality is only provisionally present. If so, the realization has a goal, which is to overcome that provisional duality. But even if that is so, we have no guidance as to how to approach the duality to gain the orientation towards unity, which is the normative end and as such requires the process of realization. In any case, realization, which is a central notion indicating the metaphysical and religious attitudes, cannot be left to itself. This in turn calls for an exploration on our part of the norm of realization within the religious realm and for reflection on the relation between that norm and the divine entity — though the terms as distinct do not conform with Buber's approach to the issue discussed.

---

* Schriften zur Kunst, Schriften zur Literatur, Maximen und Reflexionen, *Goethes Werke*, Bd. XII (München: Batz, 1981), p. 366.
† *Der Heilige Weg*, p. 51.
‡ Ibid., p., 83.
§ Ibid., p., 76.

[6]

The aspect of immediacy is present in Buber's exploration of the religious attitude even in his later writings. He says that the exclusive immediacy of the relationship between the man of Israel and God is not a *Weltanschauung*, but the primal reality (*Urrealität*) of a life relationship.* There is an immediacy in God's relation to man and world, and the norm of Judaism is to maintain that immediacy in a changed world.†, If this is so, we have to acknowledge that there is no immediacy in everyday behaviour. Rather, the immediacy is situated on the primary level of life, which in this sense is perhaps amorphous or hidden. More closely related to immediacy is what is described as feeling (*Gefühl*) and the inner correlation between feeling and the totality.‡ The connection is described as a concreteness of relationship.§ This emphasis on feeling perhaps indicates a shift from realization as a process to an attitude presented by Buber as the prominent religious attitude, namely trust.

Trust is an act of acceptance "by my entire being."¶ As we notice, in spite of the shift of emphasis to trust, the component of totality is maintained. Totality is a perspective not only from the point of view of the divine entity addressed by human beings trustingly but also of the human beings whose trust is not an aggregate of fragmentary expressions but apparently is itself a totality. It is therefore described as a "trusting perserverance in the contact".** Hence, the relation of faith is a relation of the entire being.*** The reference is to the whole life of the whole man, to the actual totality of his relations**** or to the fullness of life, the full intention of faith,* and therefore to the full dimension of human existence. There is a symmetry between the divine and human fullness, in spite of the ontological difference between the two levels.

It is plausible to assume that even in the shift from realization to trust, an attempt is made to understand the latter as a total attitude,

---

*   *Two Types of Faith*, trans. by Norman P. Goldhawk, (New York: Harper 1961), p. 130.
†   Ibid., 12.
‡   Ibid., 8.
§   Ibid., p. 131.
¶   Ibid., 6; p. 8.
**   Ibid., p. 10.
***   Ibid., p. 8.
****   Ibid., p. 41.
*   Ibid., p. 56.

and not as an aggregate of fragmentary acts. Here the shift from legislation to trust and the relation between trust and the primary position of human existence raises the question as to whether trust is a manifestation of a basic human attitude or is an attitude directed by the revelation of God, and therefore by God's presence and manifestation towards human beings. We can assume that if the aspect of immediacy is truly central, immediacy would be rooted in the human attitude as such and could not be viewed as a response of human beings to the divine presence or revelation. But these aspects are not analyzed by Buber, apparently because the emphasis on immediacy clashes with the reflective attempt to come to grips with the various components of the attitude of trust.

[7]

To be sure, there is a basic kinship between trust or confidence and faith in the religious sense because of the aspect of *"fides"* in confidence. There are certain implications in confidence related to the being that elicits trust, specifically an implicit or explicit assumption as to the points of value inherent in that being. This is certainly so within the religious realm: the divine being considered the perfect being. From that synthesis of being and value, the "ought" directed towards human beings becomes explicit. But since the explication is grounded in the primary synthesis of reality and value, trust is endowed with a cognitive component. One trusts God because one knows that God is a perfect reality, and thus, for instance, a just judge. The cognitive component comes to the fore in what can be described as the anticipatory aspect of trust, namely that the person who trusts anticipates a response from the being addressed in that attitude. The attitude of trust is not analyzed by Buber, nor are its various aspects made explicit by him, probably because he attempts to present it as an attitude grounded in feelings or in the primary reality of life. Its explication, however, is essential not only for understanding trust from without but also from within. Here once again we encounter the built-in limits of a philosophical attempt to remain within the sphere of immediacy, and even the paradox of such an attempt.

It is appropriate to refer here to the distinction between the three degrees of subjective validity of judgment presented by Kant: opining, believing and knowing. Opining is holding a judgment that is consciously insufficient both objectively and subjectively. When we hold a judgment that is subjectively sufficient but at the same time objectively insufficient, we have what is termed believing. When we hold a position taken to be true both subjectively and objectively, we have knowledge. "The subjective sufficiently is termed *conviction* (for myself), the objective sufficiently is termed *certainty* (for everyone)."* Employing these distinctions, we can ask where trust should be placed among cognitive attitudes distinguished by the criterion of validity.†

We will now proceed to consider whether the transference of the religious attitude to the dialogue between the I and Thou can resolve the perplexities of immediacy.

---

*   *Kritik d. reinen Vernunft* B p. 850; Kemp Smith transl. p. 646.
†   The attitude of confidence is dealt with by the present author in: "On Confidence", *Philosophy*, 1972 pp. 348 ff.

Chapter Eleven

Religion versus Philosophy

[1]

A critical exposition discerns the various components of its subject matter. It also criticizes, in the ordinary sense of the term, the consequences or outcome of the system of thought it examines. We have already looked at some elements in Buber's thought. We now must ask whether they are a consequence of the difference between a descriptive and a systematic approach to the components of human existence.

Having said this, we turn our attention to a systematic presentation of the relation between religion and philosophy as contradictory. One statement by Buber in particular calls for analysis, namely, that unlike dialectic, dialogue is not a privilege of spirituality. He adds further that the division in this context is not between those who are talented and those who are not. The division, rather, is between those who open themselves and those who maintain their own position. Dialogue is not a matter of spiritual luxury, but a creation of creatures. This is the main focus of Buber's exploration of the subject.* These statements are meant to point to the basic difference between dialogue, which is the medium and the content of faith or religion and dialectic, which apparently is synonymous with the philosophical approach as such. Dialogue, as it were, is given, grounded in existence as such and therefore not included under the heading of spirituality,

---

*   *Zwei Glaubensweisen*, p. 180.

whereas dialectic is a deliberate approach to existence, and thus is spiritual in a particular sense of that term.

[2]

The comprehensive aspect of human existence, the aspect essential in religion, is emphasized in the mutuality of relation between what Buber describes as what is above and what is below. The word of one who would speak to the human being without speaking with God, says Buber, does not reach the state of perfection. Yet, the word of one who would speak with God without speaking to human beings gets lost.*

We needn't delve into the meaning of these metaphorical statements other than to stress that according to them there is no legitimate way to address human existence without referring to God, but, equally, there is no way of referring to God without referring at the same time to human existence. Thus, and this has been stressed before, there are two dimensions to the I-Thou relation — that between one human being and another, and that between the human being, either in singular or plural, and God. These two dimensions are not parallel; they converge in the essence of the dialogical form, and as a result the horizontal and the vertical dialogue are conceived as one configuration.

Yet, precisely because of the reference to religion, we may ask whether such convergence is warranted or whether, because of God's initiating position in that dialogue, primacy has to be attributed to the relation between man and God. The question is essential not only because of the differences between religion and philosophy posited by Buber, differences which make philosophy a limited approach to reality described as spirit or spiritual activity, but also because of several categorial distinctions, which remain to be analyzed .

[3]

Buber says of faith that it is not a feeling about the soul of man but an entrance into reality. That entrance is said to be directed to the *whole* reality without reduction or curtailment.† Yet we cannot but wonder

---

* *Eclipse of God*, p. 152.

Religion versus Philosophy   87

as to the meaning of that entrance since the human being is already in reality in his primary situation and does not have to enter it. His thinking about reality or his discerning of different components of it do not take him out of reality. In addition, Buber emphasizes an entrance into the *whole* of reality, and the unavoidable and essential question is what that refers to. Is it the universe or cosmos at large, or is it a substance that differs from appearances? Does Buber mean a sort of cosmic loyalty in Whitehead's sense, or is he referring to God, who is a partner of a relation but is not total reality in a pantheistic sense? The question is compelled by his statement that "the human substance is melted by the spiritual fire which visits it."[*] Holding in abeyance elementary questions such as, what is the "human substance," and what is the "spiritual fire" that "visits" it, we may presumably interpret this parabolic statement as assuming that the human substance is inherently involved in and responds to relations. For were it not for the presence of two distinct poles involved in a relation, what he calls spiritual fire would not be capable of melting the human substance. Furthermore, that spiritual fire is apparently not a constant element of the relation with the human substance, but "visits it", that is to say, establishes contact with it from time to time. Buber subsequently states that breaking forth from the melted human substance are human conception and human speech, which are witnesses to Him who stimulated it and "to His will."[†] Now if this is so, then even the fundamental faculties of human existence, i.e. conception and more so speech, are not truly elements of the human partner who relates to the Thou of God, but are stimulated by Him and are contingent upon His will.

In terms of the religious interpretation of human existence, Buber probably gives priority to the human being's dependence on God and does not deal exclusively with the mutual relation between the human being and God. To be sure, there is a kind of perplexity here, since the religious attitude presupposes the existence of a being described as absolute, or unlimited and unconditional. But the unlimited and unconditioned being is not the total reality in the pantheistic sense, since other beings, limited and conditioned, exist outside that being.[‡] Moreover, within the sphere of divine reality Buber tries to find a proximity between the position of being absolute and the position of

---

†   Ibid., p. 3.
*   Ibid., p. 135.
†   Ibid.
‡   Ibid., p. 96.

being personal. The attempt to combine these two attributes is probably grounded in the attempt to maintain the absoluteness of God while placing it at the same time within the context of dialogue. A dialogue apparently presupposes the position of the person. It cannot be with the absolute because in that case the human being would approach the absolute without encountering a response. The concept "absolute" can be integrated in a philosophical system — as is done by Cusanus. The notion of "dialogue" seems to be more congruous with religion and faith.

[4]

Religion is described as the act of holding fast to God.* This description emphasizes the relation of the human being to God from the position of the human being. The emphasis is also on reciprocity, or even man's independence, which was established by God and has remained undiminished. Hence: "In this independence he stands over against God."†

The relation between holding fast and entering a relation from a position of dependence is paradoxical, even dialectical. Reciprocity and dependence are maintained as belonging to one and the same configuration though dependence implies preference of that upon which the dependent component relies.

Buber's speaks about "establishing essential immediacy."‡ That brings up the question of whether essential immediacy is encountered or brought about, i.e. established. An objective viewing, as opposed to essential immediacy, is said to bring about the situation where "we are given only an aspect and ever again only an aspect."§ The objective view, which apparently differs from full reciprocity between the I and Thou, emphasizes opposition between the partial aspect and the totality. "...It is only the relation I-Thou in which we can meet God at all, because of Him, in absolute contrast to all other existing beings, no objective aspect can be attained."¶ If this statement is valid, then the immediate relation between the I and Thou on the level of human existence is akin to the relation to God. Both defy objective analysis,

---

*   Ibid., p. 123.
†   Ibid., p. 105.
‡   Ibid., p. 128.
§   Ibid.
¶   Ibid.

which fragments the systematic relation, brings up separated aspects, and thus denies the wholeness of the relation. If this is so, in light of the inequality of the partners in the human being–God relation the meaning of the independence of the human being remains an open question.

[5]

It can be understood in this context that Buber's criticism of an analytic approach starts by highlighting the built-in limitation of reflection, interpreted literally as an attitude where a person is "bending back on himself." Reflection amounts to the extraction of "consciousness" from what is experienced in the concrete situation. Consciousness as such is not experienced at all in the concrete situation.*

Though it is not explicitly stated, reflection as an act of bending back is a phenomenon contrary to the entrance into reality. In reflection the person appears, as it were, in an isolated position, referring to himself or to his detached consciousness, which essentially cannot be involved in a dialogical situation. The lack of involvement results from the person's deliberate act of separating him or herself from the basic or primary involvement. Reflection seems to be established by an act, while reciprocity in all its dimensions seems to be given, though the religious dependence upon God makes it established. To be sure it is not established by the person himself.

This implicit criticism of reflection is also inherent in the basic contradiction Buber points to between the relation between I and Thou and the relation between subject and object, described as a "classifying elaboration".† To classify facts is to adopt an attitude external to those facts; it does not present the essence of them, certainly not as seen from the inside. There is thus a fundamental difference between the abstract concept, which is linked to an intellectual system, and "the evidence of living experience."‡

There can be no doubt that the distinction between subject and object is conceptual and therefore intellectual or reflective. Buber seems to attribute a substantive meaning to the two correlates of that

---

*   Ibid., p. 39.
†   Ibid., p. 69.
‡   Ibid., p. 14.

distinction. Yet we have to distinguish between a substantive meaning and a positional one. After all, I and Thou are not identical, they are correlated. The positional aspect of subject and object therefore also applies to them, though they are not objects as mute data. The subject is not the only one endowed with attitudes and experienced relations. A trivial example will show that the component of the relation to the Thou does not necessarily contradict the position of the Thou as an object. A physician approaches his patient as a Thou. This is the motivation behind his approach. But concurrently, to diagnose the patient's ailment and to try to heal it he looks at his patient positionally, as an object. Buber's dichotomous conception of the difference between I-and-Thou and subject and object is a consequence of his attempt to present a contradiction between philosophy and religion. Hence, what is called for at this point is a systematic elaboration of the difference between religion and philosophy. Anticipating the explication of the issue, it can already be said that while immediacy may have a bearing on faith or religion, when attributed to religion it is also a philosophical interpretation.

[6]

The dichotomy between philosophy and religion is drawn by Buber somewhat extremely. The distinction he makes is referred to as that between "totalization" and "unification", though the basic difference between these two approaches to reality is not made clear. One possible suggestion is that totalization brings the multiplicity of things and occurrences in reality under a common heading, whereas unification focuses the multiplicity on one level or perhaps within a personal God. Buber says that "...thinking overruns and overwhelms all the faculties and provinces of the person. In a great act of philosophizing even the fingertips think — but they no longer feel".* Buber seems to be suggesting by this metaphorical statement that philosophizing gives a radical priority to thinking and thus does not provide an adequate description of all the faculties of the person, particularly feeling. Thus the dichotomy amounts to that between feeling and thinking. That dichotomy in turn may be related to a rejection of any inner relation between feeling, or even trust, and reflection. Yet even such a dichotomy is grounded in reflection: the juxtaposition between

---

* Ibid., p. 44.

Religion versus Philosophy 91

thinking and feeling does not express a feeling, but expresses, rather, an articulation which in turn is provided by reflection.

To put it differently, Buber does not view philosophy as synopsis of different avenues of human activities or attitudes. As synopsis, philosophy could also explicate or articulate what is inherent in the religious attitude by applying reflection, without necessarily replacing the religious contents by substantive ones grounded in philosophy. Hence, when it is said that the believing man loves God,[*] a philosophical approach cannot avoid exploration of the difference between love as an attitude between human beings and love of God, including an explication of the possible relation or difference between trust and love. The emphasis on the contextual situations of human beings points to a multiplicity of components or aspects. What the context is has to be explicated and this can be done only through reflection. The same lack of explication leaves us in the dark as to the essence of any religion. Obviously, even highest certainty, is spoken of but what it is is not made clear, not even when that is said "that the meaning of existence is open and accessible in the actual lived concrete, not above the struggle with reality but in it".[†] "Meaning of existence" is a rather vague concept; it can be applied to suffering, which unfortunately is also a meaning, is certainly related to the actually lived concrete, and is a struggle with it. We still wonder how all this is related to "the highest certainty", unless we interpret that certainty as a sort of theodicy. These aspects are not explored or made prominent by Buber because of his tendency to juxtapose feeling with thinking. The following is a rather telling statement:

> Philosophy errs in thinking of religion as founded in a noetical act, even if an adequate one, and in therefore regarding the essence of religion as the knowledge of an object which is indifferent to being known. As a result, philosophy understands faith as an affirmation of truth lying somewhere between clear knowledge and confused opinion. Religion... does not understand it as a noetic relation of a thinking subject to a neutral object of thought, but rather as mutual contact...[‡]

The basic issue seems to be the interpretation of the noetic act, which, phenomenologically speaking, is confined to thinking in the conceptual sense or to what is described as clarification. Faith is also

---

[*] Ibid., p. 31.
[†] Ibid., p. 35.
[‡] Ibid., pp.32f.

a noetic act, and even reciprocity cannot be eliminated from the correlation between the noetic act and its noematic intentional object. Apparently, Buber here attempts not only to shift religious certainty to an amorphous feeling but also to reject the possibility of an explication of what is inherent in religious reciprocity. Thus the reliance on reciprocity as known within the human realm is taken to amount to an adequate description of religion, which by definition is directed towards what is above or beyond the human realm.

Let us examine another statement:

> All great religiousness shows us that reality of faith means living in relationship to Being "believed in," that is, unconditionally affirmed, absolute Being. All great philosophy, on the other hand, shows us that cogitative truth means making the absolute into an object from which all other objects must be derived.*

This is a telling example not of the juxtaposition of religion and philosophy but of the shift from religion to philosophy, as if religion would not assume e.g. the creation of the world or of objects. This is implied in the statement that all other objects must be derived from the absolute. If God is an absolute entity, which amounts to a affirmation of the ontological primacy of God, all objects, whether in their totality or in their particularity, are created or derived from Him. Religious attitudes themselves contain some explications, for instance, views of God as creator, judge, redeemer, etc. These are not necessarily explications in the categorial sense but they are explications just the same. Even when Buber seems to follow Pascal's juxtaposition of the God of the philosopher and the God of Abraham, Isaac and Jacob, he seems — at least programmatically — to take an extreme position; ultimately, as a closer reading of his own text reveals, he himself is unable to maintain it that position.

[7]

The interpretation of Spinoza is a case in point. Spinoza is presented as a philosopher who has undertaken the greatest anti-anthropomorphic effort ever essayed by the human spirit. His system implies a warning against identifying God with a "spiritual principle." Buber alludes to Spinoza's concept of the intellectual love of God and says

---

* Ibid., p. 31.

that the abstract nature of the concept still expresses the greatness of God in an incomparably vivid way. He interprets that love as necessarily based on the experience which, by its very nature, draws man out of the domain of abstract thinking and puts him in actual relation with the real. That actual relation is love. Buber adds that Spinoza starts not from a concept but from a concrete fact. That fact is that there are men who love God. Here Buber adds a rather significant statement, that "since His love becomes manifest in our love of Him, the divine love must be of the same essence as human love."*

It is indeed the case that in Spinoza's system intellectual cognition and its grades are an activation of thought, the latter being one of the two attributes of God known to man. The activation is a human performance. Through thinking and knowledge it provides cognitive access to overall reality, which in the pantheistic interpretation is the totality of the universe. Out of this intellectual activity emerges not only cognition, but also that attachment or awareness of belonging to the total reality referred to by the notion of love. Spinoza did not think that love is also an attitude of the total reality, which is God, parallel as it were to the human attitude to God. This is so because Spinoza's pantheistic system presents specifications or articulations — i.e. modes — within the totality. Hence human beings in their position as a mode of the totality can activate their thinking from their own vista or perspective without assuming that totality as such takes actively the same attitudes as the partial entities including the human ones. The attempt to impose reciprocity on Spinoza's system is not warranted by the content and direction of that system.

At this juncture we have to add another reservation, related to the interpretation — and that term cannot be escaped — of God as Thou, either as a projection from human experience or independent of that experience such that the I-Thou relation within the human sphere would be secondary or derivative. Within the boundaries of personal experience, everyone is an I. When one refers to Thou in the divine sense one may ask whether one's position is exclusive or whether the other human being with whom one is related is also related to God in the same way. Furthermore, when it is said that the I-Thou relation applies to God, the relation is bound to be accompanied by an awareness that the particular I involved is only a limited being vis-a-vis God. That is also the case when the given, even immediately given, Thou is another person. That is to say, the awareness of limitation or

---

*   Ibid., pp.15f.

finitude has to be stressed within that context in both directions — toward God and toward the human being. The emphasis laid on reciprocity somehow overshadows the aspect of finitude.

The awareness of finitude may yield yet another consequence. In spite of all the certainty that accompanies his awareness, the individual may be mistaken, that is to say God's relation to the human being is to mankind and not to his or her own individuality. It goes without saying that such a deistic interpretation is not a mere invention for the sake of argument. The reliance on certainty may well be a reliance on illusion. Hence, we are brought back to the main issue, namely that reflection cannot be evaded, not even from the point of view of the aspects internal to the religious attitude. The critical component of reflection is present, whether we acknowledge it or not.

[8]

Buber tries to point out some similarity between his view of love and Spinoza's concept, including *amor dei intellectualis*. But it is impossible to disregard some of the basic differences between their respective views. The main issues are the following: Buber places love within the context of reciprocity. Hence, love is a mutual attachment between the partners. Spinoza relates love to the highest level of knowledge. For him love is pleasure or acquiescence accompanied by the idea in the mind. It is an outcome and not a given affect or attachment. Intellectual love of God is pleasure accompanied by the idea that God is its cause. Hence, there is an intrinsic interpretation of what it is that gives rise to love and is therefore, categorially speaking, a cause. In Spinoza there is bound to be symmetry between love referring to God and the position of God. Love is considered to be eternal since it refers to God as an eternal cause. The eternity of God is an indication of the basic feature that love is not an attitude within the immanent human sphere but one relating man to God. The shift to pleasure as a response to the relation to God as the cause is therefore not an expression of reciprocity but an accompanying response of the affective component of the one-sided relation between man and God from the position of man.

When Spinoza refers to God's self-love, the self-referential aspect of love is but the other side of the self-referential essence of God's knowledge of Himself. God's position is of *causa sui*. Therefore God knowing Himself knows Himself *pari passu* as the cause. The human response to God as cause in the form of love and pleasure is the direct result of that self-referential aspect of the cause knowing itself in its position as *causa sui*. When God, insofar as He loves Himself, also loves man, this is not an expression of reciprocity. This is so because of the pantheistic aspect, according to which the position of man as a mode of the substance is inherent in the substance. Thus, human beings are by definition within the realm of God. Love is self-referential and as such refers to men because men are within the universe and thus within the divine realm. For men to reach the position of love they must reach the highest grade of knowledge referring to God as substance. God's love of Himself and of men is given and is not to be achieved. Hence, any alleged similarity between Buber's theory and a system based on substance, attributes, and modes, which interprets cognition as a mode of the attribute of thinking, cannot be seen as reinforcing a trend of thought all of whose attempts to refer to God remain within the human category of I and Thou.[*]

This reservation is strengthened by a difficult statement in Buber's "Nachwort", apparently in disagreement with Jaspers, namely that God's transcendence does not contradict His communication with men, who have been created for the sake of that communication.[†] The background to this statement can perhaps be interpreted as follows: human beings have been created by God and one aspect of God's absolute position is His position vis-a-vis those creatures. Be that as it may, God for Buber is a partner in the I-Thou relation with human beings. But that factual position is only a point of departure for stressing that the very presence of human beings as creatures is also for the sake of God Himself and His communication with them. In a sense, God refers to Himself because the status of communicated beings is not primarily given nor does it have a teleological meaning — i.e. grace of God — in terms of those beings. It is a status that brings even communication back to the absolute position of God as the creator of the world.

This statement leads us to wonder whether the I-Thou structure is applicable to the relation from the human being to God and from God to the human being. In the act of creation as conceived by the monotheistic religions, with all their differences, the world — including human beings — is created by the outgoing act of God as the creator.

---

[*] *Ethics*, Part V, Proposition XXXII, and further, R.H.M Elwe's translation, in *The Chief Works of Spinoza*, vol. II (New York: Dover, 1951), pp. 263ff.
[†] *Nachwort*, p. 302.

We can ask what is the reason for that act or its end. Yet if communication is for the sake of God Himself, then creation, which is the infrastructure of communication, is an act for the sake of God Himself. Its outcome is for the same purpose. In Buber's thought the communication occurs in two ways, namely from human beings to God and vice versa. One could suggest that some of the basic manifestations of that communication are prayers, man's trust in God and in His relation to human beings, which seemingly are exclusively human attitudes. In the attitude of trust or prayer man addresses God and expects a response. That attitude can thus be interpreted within the context of the I-Thou relation. But this legitimate interpretation is no justification for a possible enlargement of the I-Thou relation to that between God and human beings in general. A religious attitude is bound to be unidirectional, since it is an attitude of human beings to God, even though a response may be awaited or even presupposed. Something of Spinoza's self-referential position of God has been retained by Buber. Yet because of that this position cannot be totally or even significantly integrated within the scope of the interpersonal I-Thou relation. Reciprocity does not go along with self-sufficiency.

We can sum up by saying that by applying the I-Thou structure to the religious realm, Buber was able to identify some components of religiosity. But that identification is anthropocentric and cannot be projected onto the theocentric aspect, which by definition is essential in any religious attitude, at least in the monotheistic sense of religion.

[9]

God's absolute status, which as the notion of "absolute" implies, makes God the real being beyond the relation, undergoes a change when it is said that in order to speak to man God must become a person. This signifies an inner transformation within the divine realm, because the primary position of God as absolute does not contain the position of a partner qua person. Buber therefore adds that to speak to man, not only must God become a person, He must also make man into a person.* If this is so, we wonder whether turning the human being into a person is an additional intervention by God, or whether the human being as a creature is already initially a person, by virtue of the fact that he or she is made in the image of God. In any

---

* *The Prophetic Faith* (New York: Harper & Row, 1960), p. 164f.

case, there are apparently two steps or acts, one whereby God Himself as *causa sui* turns His absolute position into the position of person, and a second or parallel act that transforms the giveness of the human position as creature into the human position as person. Buber attempts to replace Kant's autonomous interpretation of man as a person into a symmetry between the self-referential act of God and God's act vis-a-vis the human being.

The human being's dependence on God, according to Buber, is manifested in the fact that in each Thou we address the eternal Thou.[*] Does this mean that every human being involved in the structure of reciprocity as a Thou is a partial or terrestrial manifestation of the divine Thou? If this is so we are bound to be aware not only of the Thou as a creature, but also of the notion of the eternal Thou manifested in the position of the human being. Interhuman reciprocity would thus be an expression of the vertical reciprocity of the human being and God, with primacy given to the latter.

By introducing the notion of the love of God, Buber tries to establish the position of God beyond that of an idea: God is an actuality that rises above the idea. Love bears witness to the existence of the Beloved.[†] The emphasis is obviously on existence or reality, love being an attachment, not to an idea as Hermann Cohen thought, but to a reality *par excellence*. But the meaning of that reality being absolute, and thus potentially self-referential, is not clear because of the oscillation between the supreme and thus absolute position of God, and the reciprocal involvement Buber tries to establish, or to interpret, as an essential quality of the religious attitude.

Thus we come to the conclusion that though Buber attempts to portray religion as fundamentally different from philosophy, when dealing with religion he cannot escape the introduction of philosophical distinctions. This finds expression when he attributes to God the positions both of absoluteness and of a Thou. He tries to rely on experience as an immediate encounter; accordingly from this point of view the I-Thou relation is experiential. But he also projects the I-Thou relation onto the relation between the human being and God, and the latter cannot be experiential. What is more, the position of the human I is but a result or manifestation of the act of creation, which cannot be experienced. Programmatically, Buber attempts to give supremacy to the religious attitude. But he remains not only with a duality

---

[*] *Ich und Du*, p. 19; p. 6.
[†] *Eclipse of God*, p. 62.

between philosophy and religion, but also without a coherent interpretation of religion and religiosity in his own terms.*

---

* *The Philosophy of Martin Buber*, edited by Paul Arthur Schilpp and Maurice Friedman, LaSalle, Open Court, contains articles on Buber's philosophy of religion by Fritz Kaufmann, Malcolm L. Diamond, Mordecai M. Kaplan, Emil L. Fackenheim, and Hugo Bergman. pp. 201ff. There also is Buber's, "Replies to My Critics," pp. 689ff. On the issue of immediacy, see: Kah Kyung Cho, "Mediation and Immediacy for Husserl," in: *Phenomenology and Natural Existence*, Essays in Honor of Marvin Farber, ed. by Dale Riepe (Albany, New York: State University of New York Press, 1973), pp. 56ff.

Chapter Twelve

Reconsideration

The phenomenon of immediacy, or the attitude described as such, has been at the center of this exposition of Buber's thought. To be sure, one faces the question as to the extent to which a phenomenon of this sort — precisely because it is presented as immediacy — can be described, let alone explored, analytically. Yet once an argument for immediacy is put forward, we are, willy nilly, engaged in an analysis, which brings us back to some central issues. An argument is not just pointing to.

[1]

Buber considered his approach as an attempt to record the various aspects of immediacy in human existence. He does not construct things, he says, but presents them as they are, reports life as it is lived. In this regard his thought can be characterized, as we have already pointed out, as belonging to that trend in twentieth-century German philosophy referred to, sometimes polemically, as *Lebensphilosophie*. Here *Leben* is of course understood not in the broad organic sense, but as confined within human, and mainly interhuman, boundaries. This is a limitation of the concept of "life" but concurrently an outline of the horizon of human existence.

Since the emphasis from the very beginning is on the interhuman aspect, it can be understood that Buber is essentially a social thinker who elaborates the societal manifestations of the primary interhuman dimension. In this context he takes advantage of the well-known distinction between *Gemeinschaft* and *Gesellschaft*, which he absorbed mainly from Tönnies. Buber tries to present modes of social coexistence that are primarily non-organized and non-institutional, and gave preference, both descriptively and normatively, to *Gemeinschaft*. This preference fostered a scepticism on his part regarding the political organization of social existence. It also influenced his evaluation of the political aspects of Zionism, leading him to belittle the significance of the political dimension in his interpretation of basic trends in contemporary Jewish life. Buber's favoring of the non-organized mode of human existence not only motivated him to take a polemical stance against the depreciation of immediacy in the interpersonal sphere, but also led him to what can be described as a polemical attitude grounded in his fundamental position. That is to say, we can trace a line of continuity from the immediacy referred to as *Gemeinschaft* to his criticism of *Gesellschaft* in its various manifestations, including the political manifestation. Indeed, in his eyes any given political structure is inherently authoritarian.

That set of preferences can help explain certain anarchistic strains absorbed into Buber's thinking and help to illuminate the close affinity and relationship that existed between him and Gustav Landauer (1870–1919). In Buber's view, anarchism is related to the immediate and spontaneous character of human coexistence, for existence qua coexistence is viewed by him as imbued with its own norm. As such it stands in no need of intervention, impositions, let alone compulsions, by rigid political structures. To reiterate, there is a line of continuity which runs from Buber's involvement in a theoretical attempt to maintain immediacy as he understood it in interhuman contact to his socio-political stand and to the critical or even anarchistic consequences he himself derived from that stand.

[2]

Against this background we understand how Buber moved to socialism originating in faith, that is to say religious faith (*Sozialismus aus dem Glauben*). In his adherence to socialism originating in religious faith, Buber's point of departure is not a socio-economic analysis of a social class but once again an assessment of the prospects for immediacy in interhuman contacts. In his view, immediacy stands little chance and is being obliterated under the prevailing socio-economic conditions. Socialism grounded in immediacy is seen as reconstructing the underlying fundamental human situation; religious faith complements that redemptive direction by pointing to the fact that the I-Thou relationship is not exhausted in the societal context. As partners in the dialogue between human beings and God, human beings have to be freed from a coercive and cruel societal situation that removes them from their fundamental context, both horizontally in the human situation and vertically in the relationship between human beings and the divine realm.

Zionism as Buber understood it has also to be seen in this context, at least partially. In his *Drei Reden uber das Judentum*, first published in 1911, Buber relates Zionism to the basic experiences of Jews as individuals, pointing to the duality of their experience of being at home both in the Jewish world and in the surrounding non-Jewish environment. For him Zionism is also a renaissance or activation of the particular attachment between the Jewish people and the Land of Israel. The emphasis on that attitude is probably what led Buber to write *Between the People and its Land* (published in Hebrew, Jerusalem 1945) in which he attempts to analyze the presence of the Land in the consciousness of Jews over the generations. The pivotal point in that consciousness is the primary relationship of the Jewish people to the land. Characteristic of Buber as a Zionist ideologue is his attempt to integrate additional aspects of the immediacy of human experience into the spectrum of his thinking, as in this specific case man's attachment to a place or a land.

[3]

The main theme of Buber's thought, and consequently of a critical analysis of it, is the relationship between the I and Thou and the "in-between" of dialogue — *Ich und Du* and *Zwiesprache*. These two prisms of interhuman relations, which are supplementary or complementary both in their interaction and in the systematic attempt to posit them within the human scope, may well be inseparable. To put it negatively, neither of them can be seen as enjoying primacy. Their mutual reinforcement can perhaps be illuminated by the following comment, which, to be sure, derives from a philosophical climate different from that of Buber's trend of thought. We refer to one of the formulations of Kant's categorical imperative, namely that man has to be viewed not merely as a means but also as an end. To invest a person with the position of being an end, and not only a means, one has to be aware in the first place of approaching a person and not —

to put it bluntly — a stone. Such an awareness, which precedes the exercise and application of the imperative, at least partially, is equally essential for the identification of the person as a person and for the move to the field of morality. At the same time, that awareness itself does not necessarily imply the introduction of the moral perspective expressed in the categorical imperative. The categorical imperative does more than bring the identification of somebody as a person into the scope of our behaviour in order that that person would be approached as an end and not only as a means. The moral perspective enhances the person's position as a person and at the same time it embraces what is already present in the primary awareness and identification. Summing up the interaction between the normative and factual modes of awareness, we find that the two perspectives are mutually reinforcing. That situation leads us to the phenomenological conclusion that neither perspective can be separated from the other.

With this in mind, we return to our point about the *Ich und Du* and *Zwiesprache*. It can be said that *Zwiesprache*, the in-between position, is possible only between two human beings, or between and I and Thou. That position is asserted and reinforced by the awareness of ourselves either as partners or as observers. Dialogue, the focus of the in-between situation, thus occurs between an I and Thou. When we look at the order or structure of human reality, there is no point of beginning — the dialogue emanates from the I and the Thou, and as such reinforces their dialogical partnership. By the same token it also manifests and reinforces their position as partners. A mute relationship between *I* and *Thou* would be beyond or would be preceding the scope of interhuman contact; silence relates to a dialogue and is not a transformation or continuity of muteness.

[4]

We now move to another point in our attempt to understand Buber's philosophical interpretation of immediacy, namely some of the sources of his thinking, not all of which can be easily identified textually. Wilhelm Dilthey, as mentioned earlier, was Buber's teacher, which of course is not to say that Buber was his disciple. Towards the end of the nineteenth century Dilthey delivered a lecture in which he tried to establish his own version of philosophical realism, namely a conception asserting the reality of the world. In that lecture Dilthey addressed the belief that the world exists. For him belief as such connoted the impossibility of demonstration or proof of the reality of the external world by discursive philosophical arguments. Belief replaces demonstration and proof. It has an aspect of immediacy, and in terms of its philosophical roots points to a concept employed by David Hume and discussed by Jacobi.

The aspect of belief pertinent to the attitude toward the external world is to be distinguished from belief in the sense of religious faith. In both attitudes one discerns acceptance of given facts or of the all-embracing sphere of facticity, as is the case in belief in the reality of the external world. But whereas belief is an acceptance of given data, faith implies not only mere acceptance but also trust and reliance. Nevertheless, a line of continuity can be drawn from the attitude of belief, which Dilthey advocated in his systematic thinking about the affirmation of the external world as a mode of immediacy, and the transformation of belief into faith as the mode of immediacy characteristic of Buber. Nor should we overlook another component of Dilthey's system mentioned earlier, *Verstehen*, which is also a mode of immediate awareness and understanding. Buber, it seems, absorbed these two components of Dilthey's thinking into his own, transforming belief into faith, and *Verstehen* into the dialogical situation.

[5]

Among modern philosophical trends Buber represents an approach that can perhaps be described as a phenomenology of human experience, or the interhuman encounter. It is an approach which lacks the reflection of an outside observer, who, being outside, is bound to abstract from his own involvement in the encounter as a partner. The term "phenomenology", is used not in its technical sense, since there can, of course, be no affinity between Buber's descriptions and some of the major methods of the phenomenological school, such as reduction, or some of the pivotal concepts of that school, such as the transcendental ego. Furthermore, the phenomenological school formulates its reflections from the position of an observer, who eventually achieves insight accompanied by the assurance of evidence. None of this can be found in a phenomenology of experience that seeks to articulate the experience without detaching itself from it. Indeed, no articulation, let alone explication, can nullify the conceived position of the observer. Once an observer comes on the scene, the question of distance between the experience as such and reflection on it and its presentations is inescapable. To put it differently, from the phenomenological point of view attempts to articulate experience cannot be viewed as identical with experience as such.

[6]

This attempt to understand human experience "from within" has its bearing on Buber's interpretation of religious experience, including his interpretation of historical religions, namely Judaism and Christianity. To begin with it, it may be noted that many philosophical attempts to explicate and articulate the major trends of historical religions by applying systematic philosophical concepts to them are successful, if at all, only in articulating partial aspects of historical religions. That is due to the nature of historical religions. Unlike philosophical systems, or even a philosopher's presentation of a religion integrated into his system, historical religions are characterized by a variety of trends. Religions absorb and fuse these trends without systematizing them for the sake of presenting a categorial structure characteristic of them. Hence, while consistency can be attributed to a philosophical system, it cannot be attributed to the spectrum of motives and trends characteristic of historical religions. This reservation regarding philosophical attempts to explicate historical religions also applies to attempts by phenomenologists of religious experience, which differ from the systematic articulation of religious concepts. In this context we might refer to Schleiermacher, who emphasized total dependence (*die schlechthinnige Abhängigkeit*) or to Rudolf Otto's descriptions of the various aspects of the numinous. What applies to these representatives of the phenomenological approach to religious experience, who point to one basic aspect of that experience, is also relevant to Buber's interpretation, which transposes the I-Thou encounter from the human context to the relationship between human beings and God.

Buber's transplantation of the I-Thou structure to his interpretation of the religious experience in general and of Judaism in particular, or conversely, his transposition of it from the religious context to the interhuman one, is his well-known but problematic contribution to modern thought. The problematic aspect of that two-way shift lies in the fact that the religious context is understood not as being *sui generis*, but as having, as it were, an interhuman parallel. Those who attempt to deal with experience as such without characterizing the divine realm in particular are perhaps on safer ground than Buber. The difference lies in the fact that those philosophers or phenomenologists acknowledge the uniqueness of the religious experience, even when they use the term "experience" in their systems to characterize the religious attitude.

One could go a step further and claim, paradoxical though it may seem, that because the characterization of religions — and of Judaism — calls for a separation between the human being and the essence and position of God, it found its exponent in Hegel. Hegel characterized Judaism as the religion of sublimity (*Erhabenheit*). He emphasized the fact that though religiosity involves the relation between the human being and God, the gap between God and the human being is not thereby eradicated. Because the I and Thou as involved in a *Zwiesprache* imply a kind of intimacy as well as some kind of symmetry between the two partners, the employment of those categories in the characterization of religious experience may tend to make the gap between God and man secondary. Buber was concerned with this question; he tried to introduce the ingredient of distance into the structure of the I-Thou relationship in the religious realm. Yet we may wonder whether such a synthesis between immediacy and distance is possible. Immediacy would seem to be more germane to proximity between partners than to distance between them, let alone to the ambiguous situation where proximity and distance are both supposedly present. In any case, the parallelism between the interhuman area and the area of religious experience calls for further analysis.

[7]

Buber has been received in the general atmosphere of the paradoxical "search" for immediacy. The reception of his thought is a telling example of that search (which also relates to philosophical thinking), and is related to the affinity that was believed to exist between immediacy and authenticity. There seems to be some sort of kinship between immediacy and various concepts that took hold in protest movements that adhered, explicitly or not, to the view that there is a radical dichotomy between expression and structured modes of creativity in its various forms. Authenticity and immediacy were felt or understood to be related to spontaneity. The center of the expressive attitude in these circles was the ego, its position and "authentic" manifestations. Indeed, we could say that one basic component of that drive for authenticity was an egotistic interpretation of it.

At this point we have to distinguish between Buber's conception and the reception given to it in the last generation. Buber himself did not identify immediacy and authenticity with egotistic attitudes. On the contrary, he saw authenticity and immediacy as fundamentally situated in interhuman relations. We might regard his interpretation of the phenomenon of responsibility as not fully adequate, as he stressed — as noticed before — only the aspect of response in responsibility and not the aspect of the constant personality that lies behind responsibility. Yet we cannot be oblivious to the fact that the aspect of responding stressed by Buber places the person in the framework of interhuman relations. In consequence of that, a normative anti-egotistic component is inherent in Buber's presentation of immediacy. A further consideration will allow us to emphasize the significance of this component both in itself and in the context of the "climate of opinion" of the second part of the twentieth century.

[8]

Immediacy, to reiterate, has several connotations. To focus on the notion as employed in Buber's approach we must analyze some of the meanings ordinarily attributed to the term. Broadly speaking, and from the perspective of perception or conception, immediacy connotes an awareness of reality that is based on direct contact with what is perceived. It was in that sense that Berkeley referred to perception as an immediate relation; that is to say, the bodies operating on our organs do so by an immediate application.* The things or bodies encountered have an impact on our perception or our organs by their very presence. In face of their presence as perceived there is no need or possibility for a mediation between the perception and its object.

A second meaning of immediacy stresses the absence of distance or of a lapse in time in the process of perception; or, to put it differently, the perception is instantaneous upon the encounter with the object perceived. This is similar to the first connotation of immediacy in that both connotations contain the aspect of directness, with the difference

---

* "Theory of Visions Vindicated", in: *The Works of George Berkeley, Bishop of Clayne*, ed. by A. A. Luce and T. E. Jessop, Vol. I (London: Thomas Nelson and Sons, Ltd., 1948), p. 193.

that this second meaning emphasizes directness in the temporal dimension.

At the beginning of his analysis of the judgment of taste, Kant says that that judgement is not cognitive and therefore cannot be other than subjective.* The reference there is to a judgment and not to a present object; such immediacy, being in the sphere of a judgment, is purely subjective. The difference between the previous presentations of immediacy and that presented by Kant in the context of taste is that immediacy as perception is not subjective, precisely because the relation of perception to what is present before it is inherent in perception. But when immediacy is an attribute of taste it is a characteristic of judgment and not of perception.

The context in which Buber posits immediacy is the relation to the Thou. Moreover, being immediate is juxtaposed by him with being conceived;† hence, in his view all immediately lived — and therefore real — life is meeting or encounter. This aspect of immediacy is said not to contain any preconception or fantasy — and in this sense it is apparently juxtaposed, deliberately or not, to Kant's characterization of aesthetic judgment, which contains the element of imagination. Since the core of the relation between I and Thou is the relation as distinguished from experience, the mode of immediacy inherent in it cannot be perceptual immediacy, and must be a mode exclusively specific to the relation between two human beings. What is found in phenomenological explorations of empathy or sympathy may help us to identify the specific aspect of the immediacy of the encounter that is characteristic of Buber's approach.

Sympathy is very often characterized as immediate feeling (in German, *Mitfühlen*,) that is to say, a feeling with and for the other. But sympathy or empathy is usually not presented as the basic relation between a person and his fellow man. That relation is presupposed and against it as background, or within it as context, sympathy or empathy is evoked or activated. One may wonder whether sympathy can be immediate or whether it presupposes a certain understanding of the person's situation — his grief or pain, for instance — as a condition for the possibility of evoking sympathy and focussing it in a certain direction. Predicaments like mourning and helplessness present in one's situation, would be significant both for the emergence

---

*   Kr. d. Urteilskraft, Ak. Ausgabe Vol VI. 203-204, Meredith's transl. (Oxford: Clarendon Press, 1964), pp. 41-42.
†   Ich und Du; vol. 1 p. 85; p. 11.

of sympathy, for its direction and perhaps even for the help evoked by it. For Buber, the encounter in its immediacy is the background for human relations and as such encompasses the possible foci of those relations as well as the very emergence of the various feelings between human beings. In this sense, we could perhaps understand immediacy not as an act but as a basic relation. As such it is an original or primary situation not derived from any previous context and essentially a non-reflective or non-reflected attitude.

[9]

If this is so, we may ask whether it is really possible to maintain that the relation between two human beings and between human beings and God can be understood as being immediate, that is to say, as lacking reflection or interpretation. In the first place, a relation is an isolation or separation from reality at large or reality as perceived by the person or persons involved. Even when the concept of the It is not applied or present as a latent frame of reference, the horizontal aspect of the relation is established and is not immediately given. The Thou has to be recognized as a human being and thus as explicitly or implicitly different from objects at large. He or she has to be recognized as a person and acknowledged as one. The very conjunction between knowing and acknowledging is implied in the encounter. But that conjunction cannot be immediate because the knowing may express itself in the mere awareness of the person's presence. That awareness does not directly, i.e., immediately, contain the acknowledgement of the impact of the presence on the attitude to and the response of the fellow man. The acknowledgement is both an enlargement of the cognitive component of recognizing the datum as a person as well as a focus of the attitude of mutuality. Once again, we see that mutuality is not within the frame of immediacy.

We do not have to follow Jaspers' view that human community is mediated by a reference to something other, specified by Jaspers as common ends in the world or the reference to truth and the reference to God.[*] There is no need to leap to that sort of reference to maintain or establish human community. One can discern a variety of components within the very encounter between human beings, such as the

---

* Karl Jaspers, *Vernunft und Existenz* (Groningen: J. B. Wolters' Uitgevers Maatschappij n.v., 1935), p. 51.

perception that the encountered object is a person, a specific one, one who evokes one kind of response and not another, a person met before or for the first time, etc. But discernment of this sort is not only the act of an outside observer; it is also the activity of the persons involved in the encounters at the basis of human community. That is to say, people are aware of their involvement in community, and once again it is not possible to separate the observer and the participant. Here too we come upon the problematic character of the notion of immediacy in general and of its suggested application to the interhuman relation of encounter in particular.

[10]

It is appropriate to refer now to some aspects of immediacy found in Kierkegaard. The exposition of those aspects, which are criticized by Buber himself, throws additional light on Buber's approach. Kierkegaard places heavy emphasis on the immediacy of the particular age in which he lived, and which he characterizes as the immediacy of the age of revolution. That age was restoring a natural relationship where a fossilized formalism had taken root. Immediacy, says Kierkegaard, wants to do away with inexplicables of piety and make nature the only determinant.* Furthermore, the age of revolution leads to a rediscovery of what is primarily given, namely the immediacy of the singular person. The immediacy emphasized here is not that of encounter or contact but that of the inner life of the subject, what Kierkegaard characterizes as the inwardness of isolation. It is therefore not accident that Buber criticizes Kierkegaard.

According to Buber's analysis Kierkegaard emphasizes the position of the single person; only that person can be essentially related to God. The person has to give up the essential relation to his or her fellow man in order to become the single individual and thus enter the relation between the individual and the absolute.† An additional point in Buber's criticism is that the relation to things is absent in

---

* Sören Kierkegaard, *Two Ages, The Age of Revolution and the Present Age, a Literary Review*, edited and translated with introduction and notes by Howard V. Hong and Edna H. Hong (Princeton: Princeton University Press, 1978), p. 65.

† *Das Problem des Menschen*, p. 406; p. 215. On the social direction of Buber, thought consult now: Paul Mendes Flohr: *From Mysticism to Dialogue, Martin Buber's Transformation of German Social Thought*, Wayne State University Press, Detroit 1989.

Kierkegaard, who sees them only as parables. The dimension characterized by Buber as the It is probably part of the broad context of human relations. Even though I-It relations are inferior to those between the I and Thou, they are still present in the broad framework of relations. The particular mode of relation of I-Thou as different from I-It is an assertion of a distinction and thus an outcome of reflection which cannot ignore the components of things and the attitude towards them. Observing the difference between Kierkegaard and Buber, we see that Kierkegaard is less interested in analysis of the context of relations than in the edifying aspects of his findings. Buber, on the other hand, maintains the interest in edification but attempts to place it within the context of an analysis. Thus, interpretation is essential for Buber's view, in spite of his programmatic statement which may sound sometimes to the contrary.

[11]

The verbal communication between human beings, especially that between two partners, seems to be an adequate point of departure for Buber for presenting the dialogical form of life as a fact and as a norm. The employment of the term *Zwiesprache* is an indication of its relation to the linguistic form, which is interpreted as the paradigm of interhuman relations. The emphasis on immediacy seems to be vindicated in the sphere of linguistic expression since language is activated, as it were, directly or spontaneously and can therefore be interpreted as being immediate. Yet precisely in the context of the linguistic expression it is interpretation that discerns immediacy; immediacy is not present. This emerges from the distinction between what is visibly or audibly apparent — a particular expression — and the essence present though possibly hidden.

In the first place, we have to stress the aspect of understanding, which is the other side of the coin of expression. We express ourselves, and our feelings or thoughts are presented to our fellow man. The presupposition is that in terms of understanding there is continuity between what we mean and what we say. Concurrently we presuppose that the partner in the dialogue understands, or is capable of understanding, what we say. We may even assume further that somehow both partners understand the essence of language, that is to say we express ourselves and point to things or state of affairs. Even when we ourselves do not formulate these two directions of language

— the referential and the expressive — we apply as a matter of fact, language in these directions. Hence, at least a dim understanding of what language is or at least how it operates is implied in the verbal communication between human beings. In this sense, the broad scope of language is not only cognitively presupposed by the partners in the encounter but is also inherent in it. We can generalize and say that our expression is mediated by linguistic forms and structures. To establish contact between partners a structure is required and that structure is presupposed as a background and is immanent in the communication. Were the partners only within the immediacy of the contact, they would not speak nor be able to understand. Hence, taking verbal communication as a paradigm of interhuman contact, it is not certain that we would arrive at the dialogical form — in Buber's sense — as fact and norm.

Apart from the awareness that precedes and goes beyond the linguistic expression, there is another aspect that has to be taken into account — what can be called the reservoir of language. An actual linguistic expression is an actualization or activation of the treasure of language. We are aware of the difference between the dictionary as a reservoir and our expression here and now. We draw the expression from the dictionary. This does not mean that all the items of the dictionary are present in our consciousness. Nonetheless the language latent in our dim awareness is broader than the particular expression conveyed to our partner and grasped by him or her. The two partners are aware of both the background of language and the foreground of expression. We can enlarge on this by saying that understanding in the functional sense, i.e. awareness in general and understanding in the thematic sense of what is conveyed, are interrelated. We are aware of what language is, as well as of what it contains in a more articulate way, i.e., the words and their grammatical forms and structure. This is manifest not only through the reference to the dictionary but also through the reference to the grammatical or syntactic structure of language. Hence, Buber's attempt to see a connection between linguistic dialogue and the extra-linguistic dialogical form, and a connection between these two and immediacy, does not stand the test of an analysis of the various aspects present in the linguistic expression.

To be sure, there is a connection between the exception Buber takes to Kierkegaards's interpretation of immediacy and the shift towards language, precisely because Buber stresses the openness of the individual as against the self-enclosed character of subjectivity lacking articulation. This is so since even a "stream of consciousness" has some discrete or distinct points within that stream. The mere reference to different partners in the interhuman contact already presupposes a structured contact. The I is aware of the Thou and the Thou is aware of the I. The distinction between the partners is already an articulation and an articulation is not immediately given; it is an interpretation of data. This is made prominent in the articulated distinction between I-Thou and I-It. The juxtaposition is a frame of reference and "frames" go beyond the particular components. They are — to use a phenomenological term — horizons, and the difference between horizon and the elements present in it is implicit even in our day-to-day behaviour, i.e. even when it precedes conceptual formulation. Hence we are bound to come to the conclusion that even on a day-to-day level, and certainly on the level of deliberate articulation, the focus on encounters has to lead us to awareness of what is inherent in them.

Broadly speaking, an articulation is not a deformation of what is given but a continuation of it, even when it directs us from the given to a conceptual analysis. A conceptual analysis is not an imposition on the given but an articulation of it. This is even more the case when we do not refer to data encountered through sense organs but to data encompassed in the interhuman contact. The presence of human beings carries with it the presence of their mode of existence, which structurally is an on-going conjunction of experience and interpretation. We are beyond immediacy — not by a deliberate step but intrinsically.

INDEX

A. NAMES

Bergman, Shmuel Hugo
   2 note, 19 note, 98 note
Bergson, Henri 21
Berkeley, George 106f
Berlin, Isaiah 51 note
Bloch, Yochanan 58 note
Bohr, Niels 50

Cho, Kah Kyung 98 note
Cohen, Hermann 19, 75, 97
Cusanus, Nicolaus 88

Descartes, René-Cartesius 51
Diamond, Malcolm L. 98 note
Dilthey, Wilhelm 7 note, 23f, 51 note, 61

Fackenhelm, Emil 98 note
Farber, Marvin 98 note
Fichte, Johann Gottlieb 19 note
Freud, Sigmund 27
Friedman, Maurice S. 50 note, 59 note, 98 note

Goethe, Johann Wolfgang 81

Hamilton, William 51 note
Hegel, Georg Friedrich Wilhelm
   26, 47, 61f, 79, 105
Heidegger, Martin 27, 42

Humboldt, Wilhelm 7f, 56-67
Hume, David 6-7, 52, 103
Ingarden, Roman 55

Jacobi, Friedrich Heinrich 5f, 51, 52, 103
Jaspers, Karl 95, 108

Kant, Immanuel 2, 4, 6, 13, 16, 18, 32, 40, 54, 65, 70, 80, 84, 97, 101, 102, 107

Kaplan, Mordecai M. 98 note
Kaufmann, Fritz 98 note
Kaufmann, Walter 50
Kierkegaard, Soeren A. 25, 109-110, 111

Landauer, Gustav 106
Levinas, Emmanuel 5 note
Lovejoy, Arthur G. 51 note

Marx, Karl 15
Mendes Flohr, Paul 109 note

Nietzsche, Friedrich Wilhelm 31

Otto, Rudolf 67, 104

Pascal, Blaise 25, 92
Plato 30, 31

Riepe, Dale 98 note
Rome, Sydney and Beatrice 50 note
Rosenzweig, Franz 24f, 26

Scheler, Max 12, 27, 41
Schenhaye, Margaret M. 44 note
Schilpp, Paul Arthur 5 note, 98 note
Schleiermacher, Friedrich Ernst Daniel 104
Scholem, Gershom 58 note
Simmel, Georg 58-59, 73,
Socrates 56
Spinoza, Benedictus-Baruch 26, 92f
Stiehm, Lothar 70 note
St. Thomas Aquinas 62

Toennies, Ferdinand 100

Whitehead, Alfred North 87

B. SUBJECT MATTERS

absolute 31, 32, 33, 87f, 96f
abstract, abstractness 20, 56, 89f
acceptance 71, 83, 103
accountability 55f
acknowledgement 46, 64, 109
acosmism 25
acquiescence 94
acting 2f
actuality 80
affirmation 71
age of revolution 109
alienation 26 f
allegory 33
amor dei intellectualis 92f, 94

anarchism 100
answer, response 11
answerable 47
anthropocentric 96
anthropology, anthropological conception passim

anti-anthropomorphism 92f
anti-contemplative 2
a priori 13, 66-67
articulation 112
attitude 52, 63
authenticity 105f
autonomy 97
awareness 36

beginning 66
behaviour 81
belief, believing 7, 49, 52, 84, 102
between *(zwischen)* in-between sphere passim

Cartesian direction 5f
  anti-Cartesian direction 5f
categorical imperative 101f
causa sui 94f
cause 94
certainty 50f, 57, 84, 91, 94
Christianity 72, 104f
class 100
classification 89f
coercion 101
collectivism 15f
common experience 2
common sense 24
communication 95f
community 80
compulsion 100
conception 106f
concreteness 18, 22, 62, 63, 82

confidence 75f
consciousness 3, 41, 50f, 73, 89f
construction 99
content 45, 80
continuity 47f
conviction 84
correlation 75f, 90
cosmic loyalty 87
cosmism 25
cosmos 26
creation 25, 95
creativity 105

deeds 77f
deism 94
description 53f
development 67
diachronic 3
dialectic 85, 53, 57, 5g, 61
dialogue passim
distance 105, 106
duality 81

education 15f
egotism 106
empathy 3, 22, 107f
energeia 57f
ens et bonum convertuntur 12
entelecheia 44
equality 64f
Erfahrung 57
Erlebnis 57, 6g, 76
"Eros of dialogue" 45
esse=concipi 78
essence 59
eternity 66, 94, 97
ethics 16, 33
evidence 57, 103
existence 59
existential situation 26
existentialism 39f

experience 21f
explication 69, 91f
expression 105f
   verbal expression 110
external world 5f, 40, 103

fact 81, 110
facticity 103
faith passim
fear 64
feeling 82f, 86, 90f, 107f
fiction, fictious 47
fidelity 72
finitude 94
formality 67
frame of reference 70r 112
freedom 64, 67
future 3

Gemeinschaft 99f, 151
Gesellschaft 15, 99
Gestalt 51, 59-61, 65
givenness 46, 89
God passim
grace 95
history 3, 72
homelessness 26
hope 75f, 82
horizon 112
human potentiality 31

I passim
I - It passim
It passim
idea 80, 81, 97
idea of the world 70
ideal 33, 38
idealism 33
illusion 22, 52, 94
imagination 107
immediate encounter passim

immersion 78
impressionism 92, 47f
inborn, innate 13
individual, individuals 56, 72, 94, 109
individualism 15f
infinity 67f
instinct 14f
instrumentality 64
intentionality 3, 36, 75, 76
interpretation 3f, 57, 72, 108f
intuition 76
intuitionism 20f
Israel 72
I - Thou passim

Judaism 79f, 104f

knowledge 2, 5f,
  instrumental knowledge 2
  self-knowledge 67
knowing 84, 108

Land of Israel 73, 101
language 5f, 7f, 66, 110, 11
  langue 4, 51
  parole 61
  parlance 8
Lebensphilosophie 20f, 99
libido 14
life 20f, 99, 107
  natural life 81
linguistic dualis 7f
logological 62
love 93

mankind 94
master and slave 61f
meaning 73, 91
mediation 61f
medium 7f, 52

modes 93
monotheism 95f
mortality 50, 54, 81
Mosaic legislation 81
mysterium 10, 43
mystical experience passim
mystical union 8
mysticism 25
mutuality passim

national community 69
nihilism 51 note
noema, noematic 91f
noetic act 91f
non-theoretical 2
norm, norms 3, 53, 71, 80, 81
normative postulate 44f

object 2, 51, 89f
objective perspective 59
observer 103, 109
ontological warrant 12
ontology, ontological 24, 31
openness 3, 85, 111
opining 84
optimism 26
organs 106
orientation 1f
other (the) passim
ought 12, 54, 71, 83

pain 19, 107
pantheism 80, 87, 93
participant 109
participation 22
past 73
people 72
perception 106f
permanence 72
person 2, 96f
personal 88

personalism 33
phenomenology, phenomenological approach 16f, 75, 91, 103f
philosophy 85f
physician 90
piety 109
pleasure 94
political organization 100
politics 81
postulate 44, 53
potentiality 65, 72, 80
poverty 19
practical 67, 77
prayer 96
predicaments 107
pre-knowledge *(Vorwissen)* 66
presence 46
present 47f
principles 46
process 67, 82
projection 30
proof 103
"pseudo-mystic construction" 17
psychological insight 44
psychologlcal primacy 43

real imagining *(Realphantasie)* 23
realism 21, 24f, 39f, 102
reality 46, 52, 78f, 81, 87f
realization 2f, 77
reason 19, 47
reason of the world *(Weltvernunft)* 62f
reference 110f
reflection 5f, 35f, 55f, 59, 76f, 83, 89f, 91, 94, 103, 108, 110
relation passim
religion passim

religiosity 79f
renaissance of the Jewish people 73
representations *(Vorstellungen)* 6
responsibility 11f, 53f, 106
revelation 46, 84

sanctity 67
schema 65
scholasticism 40
self passim
self-consciousness 64
self-reference 94f
sensuality 18
"sickness of time" 26, 48
silence 102
socialism 100f
society 15
solipsism 24
solitariness 42
solitude 62
space 66, 73
speculative thinking 26
speeds 87, 110
spirit 45, 65f
 pure spirit 81
spontaneity 47, 85f, 100, 105
"stream of experience" 76f
subject 68, 89f
subjective 29
subjectivism 14
subjectivity 79
sublating, sublation *(Aufhebung)* 68, 79
sublimity 105
substance 5f, 68, 95
symmetry 65, 83r 94, 105
sympathy 107f
synopsis 91
system, systems 18, 20f, 32f, 85f, 104f

taking advantage 64
taste, judgment of 107
theodicy 91
theoretical 67, 77
thing in itself 32
thinking 5f, 55f, 58, 90f
time 62, 66
time of thought 62
total dependence 104
totality 70, 78, 82, 88
totalization 90f
transcendental ego 103
transpersonal 72
trust 15f, 53, 63, 82, 96
truth 81

Umwelt 37
understanding 110
unification 90f
unity 77f

value, values 55, 83
Verstehen 23f, 103
virtues 3f

we 15
whole, wholeness 23, 40f, 66, 86f
will 67
witness 68
world 77
   world at large 36f, 70
   world environing 70
world-spirit *(Weltgeist)* 62f

Zionism 100, 101

DATE DUE

HIGHSMITH 45-220